"If anybody knows how to do it, Linzi does."
Katharine Hamnett, CBE

"An easy-peasy step-by-step guide to achiev[...]
reputation, desirability, accessibility and, of [...]
Tiffanie Darke, Editor, Style, _Sunday Times_

"If you distilled only 10% of Linzi's passion, drive, understanding and
acumen around brand building into this book it would still be essential
reading for anyone wanting to grasp the fundamentals of driving brand
exposure and fame."
Simon Jobson, Global Marketing Director, Dr. Martens

"The must-read book of the year, written by the celebrity of brands herself."
Darren Shirlaw, Founder/CEO, Shirlaws Group

"A lot of people have huge amounts of talent and ability but are not aware of
their position or potential in the market place – this book would really help
them with getting there. Linzi is one of the most enthusiastic people that
I have met in brand building and she has written a fun yet precise guide
to help you achieve the brand fame status that everyone seems to be going
crazy for."
Trevor Nelson, BBC Radio 1 DJ

"Passion, persistence, expertise, insight and energy are what's needed to
make any brand famous. These qualities are exactly what Linzi brings to her
work and in this book she makes it all accessible in an easy-to-use step-by-
step guide."
**Mike Harris, Founder, Egg and Firstdirect and ex-CEO, Mercury
Communications**

"Knowing what a talented, personable, innovative, passionate and driven
individual Linzi is, I wouldn't have expected her debut as an author to have
been anything short of a ground-breaking success. She's given the literary
world and the universe of branding an absolute gem of a read!"
Kanya King MBE, Entrepreneur, Founder, MOBO

"When I met Linzi we had an instant connection – two northern girls sat in
a room chatting as if we had known each other a lifetime. She is the only
person I have ever known to get a round of applause in a meeting, she's that
good! She recognizes the true power of fame and brand and how the two
worlds connect. Now Linzi has made it possible in her book for many more
people to experience these two worlds and she's made it as easy as 1, 2, 3!"
Melanie Sykes,

BRAND
FAMOUS

How to get
everyone talking
about your
business

Linzi Boyd

CAPSTONE
A Wiley Brand

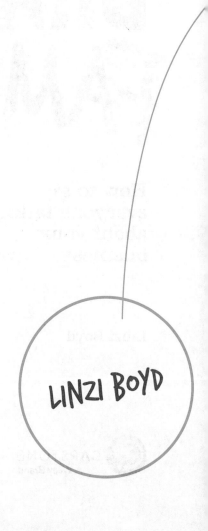

LINZI BOYD

DEAR PARTNER AND FELLOW BRAND BUILDER

—

I'd like nothing more than to walk into your office and see my book, tatty, battered, used, covered in Post-it® notes with pages ripped out and stuck on the wall – a true reflection of your efforts to develop your brand from idea through to execution. It's not just another book full of ideas to read and leave on a bookshelf, it's not a beautiful coffee table book that looks great as an ornament when people come round, it's a book written to engage you and your team to take action, working through each of the five steps and enabling you to deliver on each action to bring the method to life for your own brand.

I purposefully wrote this book to be something that acts as an extension of your brand, guiding you through the whole process over and over again, even after you have finished it. When I work with a brand I am a hands-on person with a can-do attitude and I hope it will feel like I am there with you every step of the way through my experience and with the process. I invite you to use some of the exact same tools and processes and play the same games that I would use with any brand that engages me to get to the next level and achieve stand-out status.

What is the next level? Well, to know that you need to know the level you are at now...

This edition first published 2014
© 2014 Linzi Boyd

Registered office
John Wiley and Sons Ltd, The Atrium, Southern Gate, Chichester, West Sussex,
PO19 8SQ, United Kingdom

For details of our global editorial offices, for customer services and for information
about how to apply for permission to reuse the copyright material in this book
please see our website at www.wiley.com.

Library of Congress Cataloging-in-Publication Data

Boyd, Linzi.
    Brand famous : how to get everyone talking about your business / Linzi Boyd.
        pages cm
    ISBN 978-0-857-08490-3 (pbk.) — ISBN 978-0-857-08492-7 (ebk) —
ISBN 978-0-857-08491-0 (ebk)   1. Branding (Marketing)   2. Strategic
planning.   I. Title.
    HF5415.1255.B694 2014
    658.8'27 —dc23   2014002211

A catalogue record for this book is available from the British Library.

ISBN 978-0-857-08490-3 (paperback) ISBN 978-0-857-08492-7 (ebk)
ISBN 978-0-857-08491-0 (ebk)

Thanks to ico Design for cover/page design and art direction.

Cover photography: copyright 2014 Rankin; all rights reserved.

Set in 9/11pt ClarendonLTStd by Toppan Best-set Premedia Limited, Hong Kong
Printed in Great Britain by TJ International Ltd, Padstow Cornwall, UK

CONTENTS

THE BAROMETER OF A FAMOUS BRAND

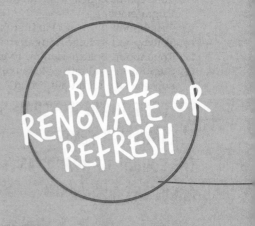

BUILD, RENOVATE OR REFRESH

Believe it or not, it's not that hard to become a famous brand and it need not take years to achieve! You will find that there are a couple of ways in which I would typically help people to assess where their starting point is for whatever stage their brand is at. In writing this book, I have drawn upon over 20 years' experience in making my own brand and the brands of others famous.

I have chosen to include two of the diagnostics that I would typically use for you to get an understanding of where you are at with your brand, so we can have a clear direction for your brand when using the process throughout this book. The first diagnostic is the "BAROMETER OF FAME". The barometer provides a high-level synopsis of what makes a famous brand. The second diagnostic is the "STAND-OUT survey", which is more of an internal measure to get a sense of what stage you are at with your brand and which areas you should pay most attention to.

We then go into your brand and actually look at where your brand is at the moment and how you perceive it. We look at what degree of fame would help you, and in order to access that fame we can determine whether you need to <u>build, renovate or refresh your brand.</u>

HOW FAMOUS ARE YOU?

—

Let's first take a quick snapshot of how famous your brand is now – if, in fact, you even have a brand at this stage. This will enable you to see where you are on the barometer before we start, as well as acting as a useful marker to refer back to as you begin the process of becoming brand famous.

If you have answered "yes" to all of these measurements of brand fame – congratulations, you are a famous brand! You now have the chance to incorporate some tips and tricks to keep your brand growing and retain the number 1 fame spot for success.

If you have answered "no" to one or more of the measurements, then this book will provide you with the methodology to really grow your brand into a stand-out status, hopefully exceeding all your brand expectations.

THE BAROMETER OF BRAND FAME

—

01. You have a recognizable name or brand that everyone is talking about.

02. You are regularly featured on one or more of the pages of a relevant print/digital magazine.

03. Your product is easily accessible through numerous retail stores, own stores or distribution networks – potentially globally.

04. Celebrities/opinion formers are using it, promoting it or affiliated with it.

05. Retail stores are championing it and making it the "must-have" item/brand and everyone wants to stock it in their stores.

06. Your high-profile events are being successfully written about through the pages of print/digital publications relevant to your industry.

07. You have a waiting list for your product lines/services.

08. You are a leader in your sector/industry and are sought after for interviews, talks and appearances at high-profile events.

THE
BIRTH
OF A FAMOUS
BRAND

—

When you began working with your brand, did it ever occur to you that your brand could one day become famous? Many people have considered fame for themselves, but fail to recognize that it could come in the form of brand fame. I know others who say that they do not want to be famous and so hide behind their brand whilst building it, perhaps avoiding the obvious steps to take their brand to stand-out.

Perhaps fame is something that you have always dreamed of but, like many, you don't have the first clue how to get it – or you put it down to "right time, right place" without realizing that working strategically on a brand can give you recognition within your industry.

Your brand may already have had a taste of being famous but has now been overshadowed in some way by new competitors. How are you going to climb back to the top again, and this time make your brand stay famous?

Perhaps fame is in the distance – you can sense it, smell it, almost touch it, then it slips away just as you thought it was within your grasp. A fall at the final hurdle leaves you stuck and you may feel like giving up.

Is your desirable brand starting to see the cracks, as many copycat companies begin mimicking what you do? Does it look like you will lose your place on the throne and another brand could take your place?

A GREAT IDEA TURNED INTO REALITY

—

We are living in a world where to achieve brand fame is not only desirable and possible but also achievable in today's world. The media, the digital era and the entrepreneurial evolution have all meant that many people feel like it could happen to them if they could just have that one great idea that can be turned into a reality.

The problem I have come across is that people find themselves with so many ideas, too many ideas – great ideas, incomplete ideas, ideas that have a shape, a size, a creative vision, an invention and then ... people find they just don't quite know what to do with them.

What if I throw you a curveball and suggest that all you need is a vision, an idea, a plan, a process and a determination to succeed?

A little bit of Branson's balls wouldn't go amiss either!

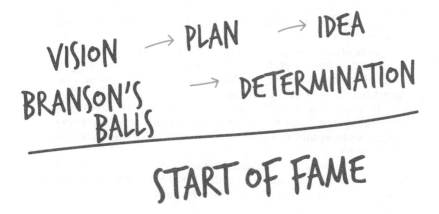

" "

What's talked about
is a dream, what's envisioned
is exciting, what's planned
becomes possible, what's
scheduled is REAL

Anthony Robbins
Motivational speaker

DO I HAVE TO BECOME FAMOUS
TO ACHIEVE BRAND FAME?

I was running a workshop recently where one of the attendees said, "but I don't want to be famous". It turned out, when exploring deeper, that he in fact felt it was very important to be known in his own business sector and when asked, further suggested that he would like to be a person of authority within that sector. Brand fame sits on a spectrum; it could simply be about recognition in your industry, unknown to the world or the other extreme, known by everybody for what you do.

As with most things in life, you have a choice. Interestingly, out of the 12 people in the workshop, 7 said that they did seek fame and 1 had never thought about it. Upon investigation, everybody wanted fame in varying degrees.

Fame with a brand does not have to be what you decide to take on for yourself, yet you may find that this is a driver for success or something that you take in your stride the more your brand grows.

HOW DOES THAT LOOK FOR YOU?

——

DO YOU ASPIRE TO BE...

——

— A market leader? Nike (the brand) – so famous, with no face.

— A thought provoker? Malala.

— A person of authority? Sepp Blatter (FIFA boss).

— A global innovator? Steve Jobs.

— A renowned visionary entrepreneur? Richard Branson.

— An influential person – a stamp collector.

All these people lead back to the same place; someone who owns a stand-out brand, product or firm, who is an inspirational leader in their industry. They often dominate their competitors in customer loyalty, distribution, coverage, image, and perceived value.

AN INFLUENTIAL PERSON – A STAMP COLLECTOR

——

There are approximately 50,000 stamp collectors known today on social media: 126,239 people and rising are also known to like this topic. Can you tell me, who is the most famous and sought-after stamp collector?

No, neither can I, but I bet you that the 49,999 other stamp collectors can.

He/she is famous, recognized, renowned; he/she might not be on the cover of *Vogue* or written about in *Grazia* magazine, but their counsel and advice will be sought in their particular stamp-collecting niche.

These people can choose to sit in a space where they are able to keep their profile intact, away from the trappings of the celebrity world without compromising the integrity of their brand or not. The decision is theirs.

We live in an age where there are people becoming famous every second along with their brand, people that you or I have never heard of, but trust me, in their field they are very influential and incredibly sought after. There are now famous bloggers, adventurers, inventors of online websites – who one minute are unheard of and the next have been valued at millions. Teenage girls have become famous by showing how to apply make-up on a YouTube video and getting millions of hits on their channel.

What a relief it is to know that we don't need to wait, sit on our ideas and think that no one will notice.

I have an idea that you have been drawn to this book. Did you reach for it off the bookshelf, drop it in your basket online, see something that grabbed your attention, or have it handed to you because you of all people are ready for action?

WAKE UP! SIT UP! STAND UP! YOUR TIME IS NOW.

What if I propose that this book will provide you with the steps to turn your great ideas into a reality and yes, create a gateway to a famous brand with you as the face in front of or behind the brand?

STAND OUT FROM THE CROWD

So, what does it mean to have stand-out success in a brand? I have found that brands sometimes feel like they need to take things very slowly in order to build strong foundations, but we are living in a fast-moving society where something that worked two years ago can now be redundant. Digital platforms that were popular two years ago, such as MySpace, have now been taken over by things such as Facebook, Twitter and YouTube. You may find that if you do not embrace the ever-changing times quickly, you will naturally be left behind.

The small-thinking mentality of a big brand with long decision-making processes could mean that this brand will be overtaken by another, smaller brand that is embracing the chances for success with quick decisions being made and multi-platform strategies being used. What worked five years ago will not necessarily work today. You need to keep looking for new ways of evolving your business. Everything is changing so quickly and your brand must do the same, in order to become brand famous.

FIRST, LET'S TAKE STOCK
OF YOUR SITUATION

— Do you have a great idea and are unsure what to do with it?

— Are you confused by all the different branding, product, marketing and PR options that get presented to you?

— Do you have a company that started out well but quickly lost its direction along the way?

— Do you still have the passion and drive for your brand but find you get frustrated with deciding which way to go next or how to drive your business forward?

— Has your business been going for a few years, with highs and lows along the way but without yet hitting the big time?

— Do you often wonder why your brand has never made it to stand-out status yet your competitors' brands have?

— Do you find yourself at a stage where you want to give it another push; however, the old ways are not working and you don't have any other options?

— Are you looking at your past success and wondering how to get back there again?

— Are you wondering how you can embrace a new process when you have tried so many times before; what is going to be so different?

Many brands have tried to achieve stand-out success using one form of engagement or another. It's not always one form of execution that brings success, but a collective of different elements working together as a strategic plan, each with a clear objective and quantifiable result attached to it so you can make sure you are getting your desired return on investment.

It's important to communicate your message through the appropriate channels, so that it is focused on what your brand values are and how to execute them, and so that you speak to your target audience from the true core of your business ethos.

Have you asked yourself what your key message and brand values are? How you want to be seen by the outside world? If you really believe that people don't judge a book by its cover, then perhaps it's time to think again?

We are living in a society where, in my opinion, a lot of people do exactly that and then care about what you can deliver secondarily. One phrase I often use is, "it's all about the packaging". Everything you put out there has to reflect outwardly in order to attract attention to its inner strengths. Looks come first and functionality second.

LB SUGGESTS

First, get underneath your brand to really work out what your brand values are. Second, look at how you appear to the outside world. Third, check that you have all the tools you need to communicate your message and that they are commensurate with your brand values. You should be aware that everything you do, how your brand looks, what you say and how you communicate it to the world is how you will be perceived.

In a world where digital has the licence to communicate anything at the press of a button and be seen by millions of people on a global scale, it becomes even more important to put out a uniform message that sticks with your brand guidelines. It is not that you cannot change the guidelines as you grow, it's just important to make sure that the guidelines change to reflect all the different platforms that you are utilizing. Your website, business cards, twitter page, video virals – everything – all have to be saying the same thing and look the same way.

If you want your brand values to reach your target audience and cement your brand into the psyche of the people, then keep providing them with the same message dressed up in different clothes, over and over again through the strategic channels that you have chosen.

From my experience, I have found that there are two types of big brand in the world today: old school and new school.

OLD-SCHOOL BRAND

This type of brand is riding on its past glory. It will have made a lot of money – enough to sustain it still being in business – yet is now actually lying dormant, unsure of its next move in an ever-changing world of communication. This type of brand normally comes in two forms:

— The stand-out big brand that ran out of steam.

— The brand that has over-maximized its exposure and ultimately ruined its reputation by being everywhere, including in the wrong retail outlets for the wrong target audience.

Both of these brand types are stuck in old ways of thinking, not reassessing their communication in terms of who they are talking to and whether or not they are still listening. Just because you were and no longer are, doesn't mean that you can't be again!

Some words of comfort if you find yourself feeling that you are sitting in the old-school camp. By following the steps in this book you will transform your brand into a new-school brand, and you'll never look back again.

NEW-SCHOOL BRAND

The other type of brand may still function as a stand-out big brand or may be up and coming en route to its stand-out status. What they have in common is the strategic evaluation of each area of the business; they know who they are talking to and what their message is, and have shared this message with their target audience on today's multi-functioning communication platforms which drive the brand forward by ensuring that customers listen.

Be clear on how you are communicating to the world.

I once went to pitch for a very big luxury brand that I would class as an old-school brand, big once and riding on the wave of their past success. They had just used an A-list star as the face for their brand and had asked me, "So what is next, who next after her?"

The brand had had a spike in its coverage and brand awareness, and wanted to know how to sustain the momentum. It had taken a nose dive; the celebrity discontinued the contract and the brand risked turning into a dinosaur. They actually wanted me to sit there and put a plaster on the situation, and give them a one-line answer instead of a strategic solution. They wanted me to tell them the next big name that would bring clients flocking.

This is the same mistake that brands make time and again – they want the quick-fix, one-solution answer and they wonder why they go in highs and lows and are not able to sustain or take ownership of their market. Spikes are great, providing high performance-related coverage and awareness of the brand. However, a long-term growth plan needs to be executed alongside this or your brand will decrease as quickly as it has increased.

It is the same as a brand thinking that advertising will solve all their problems. Advertising and celebrity placement are only two of the many ways we have to optimize a long-term growth plan. The stand-out big brands understand that to be in the top 10% of brands you have to look at more than one or two channels of communication. Your stand-out big brand will hit the desired target consumer with countless ways of communicating their creative message, making the brand so desirable that it "brandwashes" the consumer without them even realizing.

LINZIPEDIA: BRANDWASHING

—

The art of using a brand to hypnotize the consumer into thinking that investing in the brand's products was actually their idea. "I must have that product..."

"I must have that product" is the ultimate goal that all stand-out brands are able to replicate over and over again as they regurgitate creative content based around their brand values and deliver it to their target audience. Believe it or not, it's not that hard to become a stand-out big brand and it certainly doesn't take years to achieve. There are five steps that you need to have in place for you to demonstrate that you are in fact brand famous.

HOW STAND-OUT
IS YOUR BRAND?

———

Before I take you through the five-step process, let's first find out how stand-out your brand is. I have mentioned the stand-out status diagnostic already. It is an internal measurement to highlight where you are with your brand. By quickly using this diagnostic it will show you if you are indeed in the build, renovate or refresh stage. You will then be able to read on and find out more about what to do with you brand.

Answer "yes" or "always", "no" or "never", "about to" or "sometimes" to see how stand-out your brand is.

01 Do I know what the key message of my brand is and its core values?

02 Have I created a website, Facebook or Twitter page and do I have any following?

03 Do I know what my product/service offering is?

04 Do I have more than one product offering?

05 Is my product offering easily accessible through
    a. Numerous retail stores?
    b. An online e-commerce store?
    c. A service offering with more than one service?

06 Am I in more than one country with my brand?

07 How regularly am I/ is my brand featured on one or more pages of a print/digital magazine?

08 Do I have any celebrities/opinion formers using my product, promoting or affiliated with either my product or brand?

09 Do I have any retail stores talking about my product or championing it and making it the must-have product service to buy?

10 Do I host any high-profile events and are they being well attended and successfully written about through the pages of print/digital publications?

11 Is there a waiting list for my product?

WHAT DID YOU ANSWER...?

—

01.

If you answered mainly "yes" or "always", you are well on the way to being stand-out. Using the methodology in this book will refresh your brand and move it on to that next level you are craving. Good job. I look forward to reading about your stand-out status and seeing it everywhere that I turn.

02.

If you answered mainly "no" or "never", this book will really help you to create a stand-out brand. You will be able to build all the elements that are missing through following the step-by-step approach and really grow your brand through new product lines, distribution channels and marketing. You will get some great ideas on how to do this and will see a massive lift in your business and awareness of the brand.

03.

If you answered mainly "about to" or "sometimes",
you have an awareness of where you are going with your brand. You could be in the early stage of growth or trying to renovate your brand, and this book will hugely accelerate your brand to the next stage that you have been trying to get to for some time. It will give you the tools to think about what has been missing from what you are doing and engage your mind to look at what is possible and how to achieve it.

Whichever category you find yourself in, know that this book has been written so that the methodology will work for you now. You perhaps find it difficult when unsure of how to move forward with your brand. My intention is that by the end of this book, you will leave that place behind and be in a stronger position to join the dots so that the uncertainty of where to go next is removed and replaced with an awareness of what is required to deliver and achieve your goals.

In writing this book I am operating from the assumption that you are one of the three types of people whom I have consistently found myself working with over the past 25 years and, in a nutshell, you are someone who wants to:

BUILD, RENOVATE OR REFRESH YOUR BRAND

—

You may be in the <u>BUILD</u> phase; you have a great idea and want to build a brand or you aspire to get underneath your passion and turn yourself into a brand.

You may feel it is time to <u>RENOVATE</u> your brand; it is in the early stage of business with lots of opportunities lying before you. Do you find yourself frustrated that you are not maximizing each opportunity? Are you simply finding yourself struggling to take your brand to the next stage? Equally, you could be a brand that is lying dormant, having previously had all the success but struggling to move on and needing to be renovated.

You could own a brand that already has a strong position in the marketplace and just needs a quick facelift to give you the <u>REFRESH</u> you need to create new product lines, enable you to speak to a different target audience, open your brand up to new markets and elevate it to the next level.

Each road will lead to the same outcome if followed: #BRANDFAMOUS. Large or small, I don't mind. I have used this process with small brands that want to get big and big brands that want to get bigger. The thing that ties both together is that both sets of brands want to achieve stand-out status.

You don't have to own the company to drive this vision, you can be the MD or CEO of a small/big organization or even work as a team member within one. Whether you are the owner or an employee, the fact is that your unbreakable spirit will drive success and the belief that no matter what, you will find a way to make it work. I believe that how you do something is how you do everything, and the drive that makes you stand out from the crowd will create a ripple effect into the success of your brand.

Having a go-getting attitude to truly believe that whatever is put in front of you can bring success to.

Believe that you are the number 1 leading brand in your field and define everything around your business in this way. The reason for writing this book was to marry up your spirit with this book and give you the tools to create that number 1 brand within your industry. The beauty of this method is that it can become your secret weapon to succeed – you can literally engage with the process and do it for yourself!

WHAT THE METHOD IS

I am now going to provide you with my "surgical operation" – a five-step sequence I have used thousands of times to build all kinds of brands from small to big and big to bigger. If you follow the sequence in order, it will provide you with the tools you need to create a famous brand or turn your existing brand famous.

Do you think that a surgeon goes into the operating theatre without preparing what he has to do? A top-quality surgeon prepares for surgery and follows the steps with such precision that they become second nature, he hardly has to engage his brain. His primary action is simply to wash his hands and this kick-starts the flawless follow-on process. Each step is as important as the last and the next.

You are about to become the surgeon and operate on your own brand. The great part is that you already have everything you will ever need to know in this book, so here's how to put it all together.

Using the five steps ... joining the dots and communicating your message

The method described in this book has been used on very well-known, globally recognized brands over the years. Believe it or not, the process is always the same. Yes, it has evolved – especially as the digital era has come into play – and, like any method, it has grown through the years, yet the core and the fundamental architecture are still very much the same. The five steps will provide you with an overall approach to create your stand-out brand as opposed to having to apply this to every strategy you make. You will, however, also be able to apply the method to any project that you are creating throughout the year so that you get the spike you are looking for when you launch your new product or service to market.

This book has been written so that you can use each of these steps as a standalone, take-home section with Cheat Sheets at the end to keep you reminded of the key points that you need to implement. However, to create a famous brand, all five steps are required to lead you to stand-out status.

STEP 01 #DISCOVER
GET UNDERNEATH THE PASSION OF YOUR BRAND AND DISCOVER ITS BRAND VALUES AND KEY MESSAGE THAT FORM THE CORE OF YOUR WHOLE BRAND DNA. DEFINE WHO YOU ARE TALKING TO AND WHY THEY WILL LISTEN.

—

STEP 02 #CREATE
CREATE THE PRODUCT LINES AND SERVICES THAT FIT THE BRAND. PRODUCE THE TOOLS YOU NEED TO CREATE AWARENESS AROUND THOSE PRODUCTS AND SERVICES.

—

STEP 03 #CONNECT
CONNECT YOUR BRAND TO RETAIL. DISTRIBUTE YOUR PRODUCT IN THE MARKETPLACE SO THAT IT CONNECTS WITH YOUR TARGET AUDIENCE.

—

STEP 04 #COMMUNICATE
WRITE AND IMPLEMENT A 360° COMMUNICATION STRATEGY AND TAKE OWNERSHIP OF YOUR OWN MARKETING AND PR PLAN.

—

STEP 05 #EVALUATE
KNOW WHEN YOUR BRAND HAS ACHIEVED STAND-OUT STATUS BY SETTING AND MEASURING YOUR KPI AND ROI

—

HOW YOU CAN APPLY THE METHOD
—

These five steps are to be incorporated in your brand, to seamlessly go from idea through to execution. As I have already mentioned, these steps have been used successfully through my agency on brands that tend to find themselves in three categories:

01.

BU

I have a great idea

Your idea needs building; there is a place for it in this world... It is the norm when creating your own brand to use trial and error as the best way to learn how to get your brand where you want it to be. They say that it is easier and quicker to teach children than adults as they do not have to relearn old habits and they can pick things up with fresh eyes. You have a blank piece of paper with nothing to undo. You have a great idea and need help with defining what the opportunity landscape is and what you would like it to stand for.

I have a passion

You might be a person that has a passion for something, yet you are not sure how to turn this into a brand, how to create a unique point of difference so that it stands out from the other brands in the marketplace at the moment. You may already be well known but not yet have created any product lines or anything resembling a brand around your fame. Are you at the tipping point of success and you don't want to see yourself go into decline? It's time to build your brand.

02. RENO

I am in early growth

You may already be aware of who you are and what you are selling, but there is perhaps not yet a strong architecture around your brand that you have clearly defined. When you know exactly who your target audience is, you can then determine whether your current product lines/services actually connect with the end consumer. Once you get clear on which product lines will provide you with short-term and long-term gain, you'll be in a better position to become known as a recognized brand in your field.

VATE

My brand is lying dormant

If, however, you are a brand that has experienced huge success but is now struggling to tick the famous brand checklist provided earlier, then your brand is what I describe as lying dormant. You are in essence unsure how to make a comeback. You need to look at your brand with fresh eyes; take an unemotional look at who you are as well as who you are not and, importantly, who you want to be so that it is not just guesswork.

03. REF

I have a successful brand and need to keep it that way
You are at the top of your game and need to keep the brand there; you have the added pressure of being the owner of the business or the MD or CEO and are answerable to the board or team around you if the profits or awareness drop for any reason. You want a more rounded way of thinking, and fresh or creative ways of looking at your brand and instigating new ideas into your product/marketing plan. You need to be able to create a new consumer base whilst maintaining and growing your existing one – all without alienating your existing loyal customer support. This will require you to think outside the box, logically and creatively; to analyse the approach that you are taking, and maintain and grow the strong foundations that you have laid.

RESH

I want to reposition my brand and raise its profile
Finally, perhaps you want to get your business to the next level. This might mean looking at what great product lines you could produce outside your traditional offering and how you can then create a communication strategy that will engage new and existing customers. You want different ways of looking at your brand and different options for manufacturing, connecting to retail and engaging with the end consumer to guarantee a return on investment that will take you to that next level and raise awareness around the brand with an influencer audience.

WHAT YOU WILL GET FROM THE METHOD

I have always been aware that as a famous brand there is a criterion that needs to be met so that you know you have reached your final destination. When you want to lose weight you have to weigh yourself, take measurements and write down what success looks like for you – losing 2 stone, fitting into that dress you saw in the shop window, etc. There are obvious degrees of success that come with the territory so that any brand knows they have arrived when they make it to the success stage.

66 99
—
When you are a stand-out brand you will no longer have to fight for a place in the market, you will simply take ownership of the marketplace.

You will be driving sales effortlessly through the stores or e-commerce sites and will have celebrities and key people of influence vying to work with or collaborate with you and your brand. You will be in the top 10% of brands, not reflecting the state of the economy or blaming the world's economic climate or recession for your brand not succeeding.

A stand-out brand taps into those channels of communication that their consumers access, so that the brand consistently and persistently engages the target market with a succession of creative flowing content to keep them excited, engaged and more importantly investing in the brand. They have journalists from the publications read by the target audience using, wearing or trying their product so it ends up in the magazines, newspapers, online pages and blogs whilst the celebrities, idolized by the target audience, are pictured with the product in the same publications.

Your Facebook will be alive with secret offers, and you will be following them on Twitter so that you can find out where the limited-edition products are being sold through exclusive retail outlets or pop-up stores.

Start to prepare your mind for fame and success. You should create a list of things to be aware of, which will enable you to set your own goals and parameters of success so that you will know when you have hit brand fame. The road to follow was a journey worth taking when I started on my right of passage at the age of 18. The one big difference is that there was no digital era then, making today's trip a fast track to #BRANDFAMOUS and ensuring you and your brand stand out from the crowd.

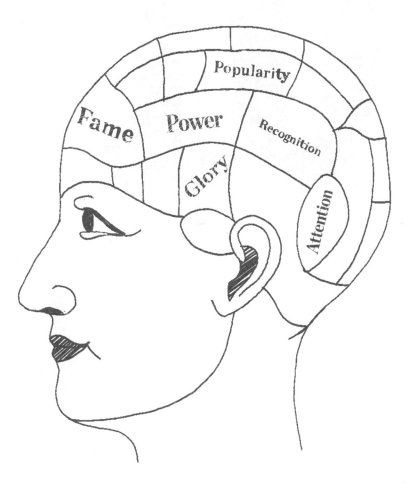

PART

01

STANDING OUT FROM THE CROWD

—

CHAPTER 01:
BRAND FAME IN THE MAKING?

___

44 77

**Becoming brand famous
is like becoming a celebrity
in your own right – everyone
wants it, people are talking
about it, they want to own
a piece of it, people try to
copy it, wear the same clothes
as it and copy the hairstyle!**

"How on earth did you own three successful companies all be-fore the age of 25 when you dropped out of school at 15?

Surely you needed to study public relations at university for three years or more before setting up a PR agency? Are you sure you knew nothing about PR? Really?"

Always having a can-do attitude was the biggest asset I had to become a big success. I have always had a strong belief – and today it's stronger than ever – that I am going to be huge: "Bigger than Oprah Winfrey" I used to tell my mum, aged 11! She would just stand there, looking at me in disbelief. I always figured that talent is one thing and big vision and determination another.

You don't have to be the most talented individual or the cleverest person to be the biggest star

Madonna, Brad Pitt, Richard Branson; each an incredible character. You probably wouldn't say that they are the best at singing, acting or business yet they all have the same star quality with an absolute determination to succeed. They are stand-out in their own industry.

In this day and age it is easier than ever before to become a big brand by the way you look, talk, do and act. Your actions will define the things you produce and your efforts will make up the blueprint for what you ultimately deliver. Your thinking and the way you act will define a big brand belief system. The world is changing – in fact, the world has changed; print, digital and even celebrity branding has become ever more accessible to smaller brands, giving you the opportunity to play a bigger game and beat the big brands and their multi-million-pound marketing budgets.

Times are changing quickly, and if you don't move with the times you'll invariably move backwards relative to those whose thinking and actions move quicker. Your new can-do attitude will inevitably redefine your thinking, facilitating the progression of your brand from insignificant to stand-out status in an effortless transition.

The biggest mistake people make is thinking that because they are small they have to think small

Take it one step at a time, don't rush, businesses should take 10 years plus before making it to a reasonable size. Rubbish! Believe that you are big and you <u>become big.</u> Thinking big is the first step to becoming a big brand. You started your own company. You leapt out of the frying pan and into the fire, didn't you? Now see it through. Why waste your time plodding along? You may as well have stayed in your dead-end job. The reason you started on the journey to set up your own company must equally be the driver for turning you into a big brand now. My story is no different from yours, except I believed that I could make it big and I could make it fast…

MY STORY

Business No. 1: Clothes shop, age 16–20
I left school at the age of 15 and by 20 I had moved to London after selling my first business, a ladies designer clothes store based in Leeds, to my then business partner. I ran the store successfully for three years and during that time I travelled far and wide (for an 18 year old) – buying in London, Paris and Milan – and successfully launched Diesel and Replay for women into the North of England. Imagine how proud you'd feel if one of your children managed to pull that off.

Business No. 2: Footwear brand, age 21–25
My second company saw me team up with a very successful footwear designer, Justin Deakin, and launch a footwear brand named Stride. We exploited a gap in the market to produce trainers that were, for the first time ever, not sports related. That, for me, defines big thinking and finding a niche. At that time, Nike and Adidas were known for producing sports-related products and we felt there was no other major competition. We sold 150,000 pairs in our first season. We manufactured the product in Korea and in three years we had 7 distributors selling them through a global distribution network across 10 countries worldwide.

Both the shoes and the advertising campaign were featured at the Design Museum, London, as design classics next to the Evian bottle and were worn by the likes of Robbie Williams and the Beastie Boys for free "because they wanted to". No money changed hands.

So, few brands were even thinking about celebrity placement like they are today and it was a key element that made the difference between us being a small brand and a stand-out global brand.

Collaboration success
We collaborated with a high-profile design company who made inflatable furniture (you may or may not remember the very famous inflatable armchair) and patented inflatable flip-flops. Did they sell like hot cakes? You bet they did – globally! Each season we had a waiting list for Stride shoes in the retail stores, with styles selling out before they hit the stores.

DID THIS BRAND MAKE IT TO STAND-OUT STATUS?

THE BAROMETER OF BRAND FAME – STRIDE

01. It was a recognizable brand on a global scale, being sold through 7 distribution channels with over 150,000 pairs per season being sold in multiple middle and high-end retail stores.

02. It was regularly featured through multiple publications on a global scale with interviews with the designer taking place in many countries.

03. There were events taking place all over the world, with distributors hosting huge parties to launch the shoes in their territories.

04. Waiting lists for the shoes were accruing in Japan, the UK, Germany, Australia and Scandinavia, with increased demand and repeat orders.

05. A-list celebrities and opinion formers all over the globe were spotted wearing them, talking about them in magazines and recommending them.

06. Magazines and publications were writing about them as the must-have items of the season.

07. Interview requests were coming in thick and fast from global publications.

08. The brand was a pioneer of fashion trainers that changed the way people thought about fashion trainers being worn.

Age 24, we sold the company to Caterpillar four years after launch date.

I set up my third company, the Surgery Group, just as many people are leaving university and sending out their CVs for a work experience job. I literally decided that I would be good at PR and yes, you guessed it, went ahead and set up a PR business. Had I ever worked in an agency before? No. Had I ever done PR? Yes, of course, every day for the last seven years owning two brands. I had to, didn't I?

I saw a gap in the market for an agency that was down to earth, normal and would produce exactly what it said on the tin, offering great results in a straightforward way. Most PR agencies at the time were all about the "it" girls, wanting to party without producing results for their clients. Instead of Absolutely Fabulous, we would be Absolutely Effective (whilst naturally being fabulous at the same time). Surgery has evolved over the last 15 years, from a small, one-man-band PR and marketing agency into a 360° full service communications agency.

We represent small unknown brands in BUILD that are unsure of their market positioning, pricing, key message and core value through to brands that know they have a great product and have no idea how to take it to market through retails and marketing/PR. These brands range from beauty products to interior designers, restaurant owners and electrical products. We have even worked with an accountant on how to make him unique and stand out in the marketplace. Bigger, well-known brands that are either in RENOVATE or REFRESH have ranged from high-street fashion/retail brands such as Urban Outfitters, Miss Selfridges through to Superdry, Aldo and Lacoste; as well as prominent food and drink brands such as The Savoy Hotel and even a whole country – Malta.

Business No. 4: Midas turning celebs/entrepreneurs into brands

I started my fourth business Midas, which is my latest venture, to enable me to incorporate the full methodology written about in this book. When working with any brand, to achieve brand fame status it is easier to build, renovate or refresh the brand when systematically walking the brand through each of the five steps incorporating the whole process. Midas is able to get involved in the creative vision/ brand positioning piece and product creation before handing the project over to the Surgery Group agency who then delivers the communications plan and engages the retailer to buy into the project.

CHAPTER 02:
WHAT'S HOLDING YOU BACK?
—

You can stand out from the crowd and so must your brand

WHO PUT THESE OBSTACLES IN THE WAY OF MY FAME?
—

The day that you made the decision to give your brand a big kick up its bum and leave the old-school way of thinking behind was the day that you chose to stand out from the crowd. Taking that leap of faith into the unknown was in fact a huge acceptance of the fact that you are now part of a new era of modern-day business thinking.

First, let's take a look at the things that prevent people from taking the leap towards being brand famous. These are the obstacles that I see as being prevalent among entrepreneurs, business owners, CEOs, MDs and anyone trying to grow their brand, regardless of how intelligent, passionate or committed they are to their work. If you cannot overcome the obstacles that follow then you could find yourself – as many do – struggling to move forward with your brand. They may seem massive to you, and small to other people. What's important is how you deal with them.

LB SUGGESTS
—

Take a moment to think about what has prevented you in the past from taking huge strides towards your stand-out status. It's likely, if you are reading this book, that you are not there yet and what I want to know is, why not? What is holding you back?

Write down the six things that get in the way of where you want to be and any obstacles that are holding you back.

FIND YOUR DOT!

—

Here are the <u>six most common things</u> that I have come across, which disrupt a brand's flow as it attempts to grow. They are all common obstacles that people could face at some point, but don't worry – there is an easy way around them if you follow the process in this book.

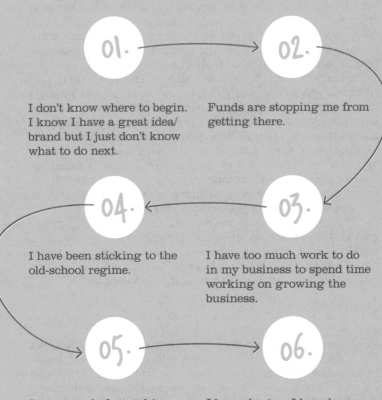

01.

I don't know where to begin. I know I have a great idea/ brand but I just don't know what to do next.

02.

Funds are stopping me from getting there.

04.

I have been sticking to the old-school regime.

03.

I have too much work to do in my business to spend time working on growing the business.

05.

I am scared of stretching into the unknown and am always waiting for the perfect time to make things happen.

06.

I know best as I have been doing this for years.

DOT 01: I DON'T KNOW WHERE TO BEGIN – BUILD

I know I have a great brand but I just don't know what to do next

I once sat with a group of business owners who had come together to get underneath their business models and their brands – one of them did not even realize that she had a brand and could easily have missed out on simple ways of maximizing her brand, and yet to me the possibilities of her brand were endless. Each of them was typically keen, focusing on getting published and drawing up product ideas to leverage their brand, and yet there was an underlying sense of fear between them which showed that, despite all their passion, they had overlooked just how special or valuable to other people their brand could potentially be. The fact is that they had no idea how on earth to implement their fantastic idea.

It's most likely that you are sitting on a gold mine, just like these guys were, and you just don't know how to leverage it. You look at other people's businesses and think that yours is just average in comparison. One of the guys in the group above actually declared, "Wow, your brands are so much more exciting than mine" and yet when I looked at his brand, as with everyone else in the group, I saw pure gold. Whether an interior designer or an accountant, you all have a story to tell and a package to wrap it up in with a massive bow tied around it – a metaphor for you going that extra mile.

There is no ordinary business out there, only basic strategies lacking structure, direction and creativity. You live in a world where anyone can become a brand in an instant. Internet and high-speed communication enables you to communicate with anyone in any country at the press of a button.

The only thing that is stopping brands from making this happen is the people behind the brands. It's time to make a change...

In the last century, before the digital age came into effect, small and large brands were reliant on a much slower form of communication. Up until the late 1990s, print and TV were the main channels of communication with many brands relying on the expensive commodity of advertising in magazines and on billboards as their main source of budget spend with the goal of raising revenue. Compared with today, that's like communicating with smoke signals across a valley!

To go global for any brand size has never been so easy.

LINZIPEDIA: DIGITAL

An online creative solution that can be featured in blogs and Internet-based publications or executed through your social media platforms. Less expensive, and increasingly effective.

A small brand has all the opportunities to go global. Since digital came into play, it has given the smaller brands a chance to reach out to a wider audience on a global platform and speak with a voice of authority through multiple integrated touchpoints. Never has a small unknown brand had so much opportunity to go up against a big force brand with multi-million-pound budgets and be a threat to their share of the market. One idea can be channelled through a variety of platforms to speak to the end consumer on several levels, so that it generates interest and leads to a sale. Small brands find that multiple sales are generated without the added cost of advertising.

DOT 02: FUNDS ARE STOPPING ME FROM GETTING THERE – BUILD

I have brands that come to me with next to no money to spend on an event or creative solution for their business, yet there is always a way of creating an experience for your brand with a minimal budget. Make something happen out of nothing – you just have to find it.

When I first opened the doors to Surgery, I worked with a world-famous product designer for a number of years called Marc Newson. At the time he wanted to do a book launch and the publishing house had £2000 to spend on the event. For a world-famous designer, an event budget of this amount was not going to live up to Marc's superstar status! I managed to raise £30,000 by persuading all of his product manufacturers to provide me with a small amount of money to promote them through Marc's book. The launch went ahead at a mansion house off Harley Street, London, with a documentary filmed by BBC1 showcasing how I launched the event and how I achieved the star-studded attendance that was present on the night. Did the book sell out as a result of all the publicity on the night? Of course it did. Next time you face this obstacle, instead of saying "I can't afford it", ask yourself "How can I afford it?" The solutions will come at you from all directions.

www.surgerytv/Best of Britain; watch the video of the event.

TIP

Resources find a way of making an appearance after commitment has been put in place.

We are living in an age where to play big is easy

Since 2000, search engines have become more powerful and research and information are easier to access. From 2005 onwards, the world of social media and the multiple platforms available to you and your business mean that you can be a global brand at the touch of a button. What's your dream? Your own TV channel? A global shop window? A huge interest in what you do, talk about and represent? Now it's possible to have all of this at a low cost to the business: your own TV programme, your own magazine. You can self-publish your own e-book and distribute it through your online shop; you can generate your own networking community to chat about your brand and target specific people who are interested in your brand without wasting money spending big budgets on advertising (where 90% is wasted anyway by targeting the wrong people); and you can even save money on your bus fare to work as you no longer actually need to leave your home!

DOT 03: I HAVE TOO MUCH WORK TO DO IN MY BUSINESS TO SPEND TIME WORKING ON GROWING THE BUSINESS – RENOVATE

I once sat with a guy who had a small business with four members of staff; he was complaining about not having the time to get things done. I sat there listening to him, whilst wondering what he was really doing on a day-to-day basis. I got him to prepare a very simple spreadsheet with every single heading that was really important to him in his work – there were 10 headings. We then listed what there was that needed to be worked on by him and what actually could be farmed out to other people – 80% of his working schedule was easily farmed out to freelance consultants who were very keen to work and help his business grow; the remaining 20% he was able to get done. This led to an 80% increase in turnover.

By stepping away from the business and detaching yourself from your everyday regime, you will be able to see the picture more clearly and not get bogged down by the details. You will see the actual work that you need to do that will benefit the growth of the brand and the work that can be done by other people. This will then give you the space to be creative and love the job that you started out to do and not get drawn into doing things that are not your passion. Once you have created this structure in your business, you are then able to delegate out the work that is not your strength and fall back in love with the side of your business that is. You can be the master of your ship, driving it forward to exceed all your expectations.

DOT 04: I HAVE BEEN STICKING TO THE OLD-SCHOOL REGIME – RENOVATE

One of the biggest mistakes I have noticed from my own experience is that brands are not seeking to discover new ways of working with their product lines in today's world that give them the tools to create the stand-out status they have always wanted! I am grateful you have picked up my book as a resource to achieve this, as we need more stand-out big brands taking up their rightful space within the marketplace.

What is a dinosaur brand in the making?
Many big brands that were stand-out in the 1990s found that they were slowly turning into dinosaur brands. Why? Because they didn't move with the times; smaller brands who engaged in faster levels of communication began reaching out more easily to a wider audience with lower costs of execution to make rapid growth a reality, leaving the once-big brand behind. This previously big brand could be a sleeping giant or on the brink of extinction.

Richard Branson was quoted as saying that "fortunes are made out of recessions". Should this not redefine the thinking behind any brand? If you and your brand move forward with the times you will never have to think about recession, you will be making so much money from your stand-out brand that you will be able to laugh in the face of recession. Never stand still. Keep on moving, otherwise you will go backwards. Recession is a mindset that simply holds you back. Imagine if governments could let go of the old ways and move on...

There are stand-out brands that have been around for over 20 years, such as Nike, Virgin and Apple, and these are the brands that have continued to evolve and adapt to the times as the years roll by and are now fully embracing the new age that we live in. Today provides you with a communication platform which, for brand building, offers a multi-dimensional platform so you no longer have to rely on using a single communication process. Look at what has happened over the last 10 years in the world.

Do you wonder where we will be in the next 10 years?
Move with the times now before someone else in your sector does...

Recently, the app revolution and mobile media have changed everything again. If you don't move with the times your brand starts to lie dormant, and it could eventually die off.

However, this is not a lesson in social media or persistence, more a five-pronged approach to maximizing your brand and moving with the way of the world so that you are not left behind with the dinosaurs. As long as you are prepared to embrace change, move with the times and follow the solutions laid out in this book you will keep your brand moving towards success and lead the way rather than following the crowd.

DOT 05: I AM SCARED OF STRETCHING INTO THE UNKNOWN AND AM ALWAYS WAITING FOR THE PERFECT TIME TO MAKE THINGS HAPPEN – REFRESH

This is the most common mistake that I hear time and time again – fear of the unknown. How do you feel when you need to move house, fearful yet excited? When you had to change schools, fearful yet excited? Similar feelings rise up time and time again; just because you are an adult they don't go away. What may be worth considering now is that if you face the fear head on there will always be something amazing waiting for you on the other side. The unknown does not really exist, the stories you make up about the unknown do. Why not just invent better stories about how amazing it will be when you do X, Y and Z in that unknown space! You know what to do, you always have done. You just need to take that leap of faith into the beautiful unknown – each time asking yourself "what is the worst outcome that could possibly happen?" and trust me, it is never as bad as your monkey mind makes it out to be.

My own agency went through a huge change a few years ago when I realized that print media and PR alone were not the way forwards within our industry – I had to take a leap of faith and employ people to run a digital and celebrity/events division without really having knowledge of where the markets were heading. We did it anyway and it quickly paid off; we were in a position to turn even more brands into stand-out big brands by being able to create a 360° communications pro-gramme when other agencies were still looking to traditional PR as the only way forwards. Thank goodness we took that leap into the unknown...

Instead of standing still and thinking small, there's now a need to engage with a new way of thinking. This means taking small steps rather than no steps, leading to big strides forward due to the high impact of what can be done in today's brand-building world.

SMALL STEPS = BIG STRIDES; SMALL THINKING = NO STEPS

DOT 06: I KNOW BEST AS I HAVE BEEN DOING THIS FOR YEARS – REFRESH

This one makes me laugh the most, as people pay thousands of pounds for a PR, marketing or branding agency and then don't want to change/refresh anything in order to improve their status quo. I cannot tell you the number of brands that have come through my door, asked for help and yet when I give them what they need they don't want to listen.

I have a very good friend who has worked alongside dif-ferent brands for a number of years – he was the owner and founder of a very famous footwear store. He once wrote a mar-keting strategy for a very well-known footwear brand that was lying dormant and in need of help to move the brand forwards. They chose to ignore everything that he suggested doing to turn their brand around. A number of years later he was called in again to chat with the new owners of the same foot-wear business that had picked up the brand which was still lying dormant. He presented a marketing strategy to the new owners who loved everything that he had written. When the meeting came to a close he laughed and turned over the strat-egy and there was the date from five years previously when he had presented the exact same strategy at the last meeting!

Are you spending money in the wrong areas?
Brands that don't refresh their business think that they need to throw more money at the situation to make it work. The problem is that they could be throwing money at the wrong areas, for instance employing a team of people to help them grow and not listening to the advice they have paid for (crazy).

They could seem to remain set in their ways, fearful of change and not bold enough to invest money in alternative areas that are new to them. Sticking with old methods is common, yet we see that the old methods are not working today.

Rather than embracing change, they could repeat the same mistakes over and over again and although they are ahead of their game at the moment, they may begrudgingly wonder why smaller brands with much less budget are driven to succeed where they are failing. Instead of jumping into massive advertising budgets, what about getting creative and producing an experience that could be filmed and written about in a press release with images attached. This can then be sent in to journalists, thus grabbing the attention of different media publications and online titles which will generate the desired reach that you are looking for from an advert yet in a more targeted and impactful way. This is a great way of speaking to your target audience or even helping you to reach out to a new one.

Embrace the new age and always challenge your brand. Take it to new heights that you never thought were possible and set goals which, conventionally, are unachievable whilst pushing your boundaries to reap the rewards for efforts made. Open your mind, reach for the impossible, set it as clear as day and know that no idea is too big – providing you create the necessary steps to get there.

My agency has spent the last 15 years working alongside brands and seen many different types of obstacle appear. We have worked together with them to overcome all types of challenge presented and create effective forms of communication to engage with the customer and bypass the obstacles. One of the most noticeable challenges presented to brands over the years is creating ways for a brand to evolve and continue to engage with their customer by using the different forms of communication tools and platforms available. In an ever-more saturated market a brand needs to stay ahead of the game to create loyalty and a desired following. The need to produce sales, deliver engaging conversations with a community and ultimately either turn their brand into (or maintain a position as) a market leader in the world now has multiple options and solutions.

You are probably aware of the fact that most of these obstacles lie mainly in your head. You built them up. Imagine how good it will feel when you knock them down. What is the ultimate thing that is going to stop you from achieving standout brand status? Your own monkey mind; if you can shut the monkey up that drives you mad in your head and know that you are part of that elite 10% of the population that believes you can achieve, then achieve you will.

Passion is one of the main ingredients – if you don't have the passion for your business and what you do, you will not get out of bed in the morning.

Commitment and determination are the second ingredient, and a great product/service is the third. However, if you have a great product/service and still do not know who you are targeting, the chances of getting off the starting block are small. If you can commit to achieve and succeed, trust that everything else will take care of itself.

Imagine how big your brand will be when you implement the changes I am going to suggest, or imagine what will happen to your brand in the event of you doing nothing more than what you are doing today and have done every day since the birth of your brand. The worst-case scenario, if you are honest with yourself, is standing still. And to stand still in today's fast-paced business climate is to move backwards relative to everyone else.

PROBLEMS ARE A CHALLENGE THAT YOU BELIEVE YOU DON'T WANT TO HAVE...
FACE THEM HEAD ON ENGAGE, EMBRACE, LEARN, OVERCOME AND GROW SHINE WITH YOUR BRAND AND EMBRACE A NEW CHALLENGE EVERY DAY!

CHAPTER 03:
HOW TO MOVE FORWARDS

THE INSIDE GUIDE TO PROMOTING YOUR BRAND

This chapter offers a quick insight into the world of promotion, so when you start the process laid out in this book you shouldn't be starting from a place of little or no knowledge when it comes to what is actually needed to raise awareness around your brand. I aim to provide you with the basics so that you can make informed choices on what it is you want to gain/achieve through the promotion of your brand.

By providing you with some examples of both old- and new-school ways, I hope to highlight different outcomes that can be achieved for any brand size and provide options that you could use to drive your brand forwards. Without this knowledge it is a bit like going on your first driving lesson without an instructor in the car giving you the basics. You'll get there in the end, but the journey could be fraught with hard knocks.

WHAT IS ALL THIS PR JARGON?

I often hear people referring to marketing and PR as if it were another language, confused by the unlimited possibilities and costs that are often presented to them and not quite sure which direction they should go in. Brands often find themselves either overspending or underspending from sheer uncertainty over what best fits their brands and they often leave it in the hands of their advertising, marketing or PR agency to create the complete vision that will then dictate the direction of the brand. Wouldn't it be great if you could take back some of the ownership and sit in a space where you were able to steer your own ship, knowing with conviction how and when to spend your money and having some idea of the return on investment you would get from the money spent on projects.

Let's start with the basics of three very clear areas that are always referred to when people start thinking about promoting their brand, which let's face it happens to us all.

Advertising vs PR vs 360° communication

Advertising has always been used as one of the key drivers of big bang brand awareness for the medium to large-sized brand. Adverts do have a place in this world, but only as one of many options available. Old-school brands need to view advertising as a tool in the box and not the only solution for generating business. Combining a 360° communication strategy with an ad campaign so that it also leverages on execution through more than one channel (in this case a billboard and/or the page of a magazine) is a definite key option to consider.

Is the power still in advertising?

Advertising done correctly can be effective but, like anything else, can equally well be a wasteful resource. You may know that placing big adverts in multiple media outlets such as print, billboards, the sides of buses, etc. is a huge expense and one that is not directed to a selective target audience. It has been suggested that 80% of your spend on advertising budgets falls on deaf ears. Much like watering the garden and 80% of the water falling on the patio!

The common mistake that old-school brands make when advertising is to use it as an isolated form of communication, not linked to a strategy, in the hope that it will turn them into a stand-out brand overnight. For instance, advertising in a newspaper will have less reach than partnering up with the newspaper to create a win:win scenario for both of you. Think about what kind of collateral you have that is a desirable asset to that newspaper. For example, do you have a huge database that hits their target audience? Have you got a retail portfolio in which you could promote their publications?

How does that reach out to more sales though? By offering the publication something that it wants, you can partner up with them so that they can then provide you with a bigger offering through the pages of their paper/magazine in the form of an editorial piece/competition or reader offer which is 10 times more valuable than just placing an advert. It also builds up a relationship between your brand and that publication, so that they start to use your product on other pages in their publication through PR which you don't have to pay for.

The old-school approach can run into millions of pounds once the full advertising team has been involved, shooting, creating and placing adverts in multiple publications. In contrast, the new-school way costs next to nothing in comparison to create a win:win situation that both you and the publication can reap rewards from. What is the return on investment from the old-school advertising spend?

Has the advertisement translated into sales? Has it had the impact of a creative viral, whipped up thousands of fans or generated awareness of you and your brand for future sales? Normally, the return on investment is a huge disappointment; when you have given a large percentage of your marketing budget to produce and place an ad campaign that returns very little, the feeling is not very satisfactory to say the least. What if it had been approached a little differently?

The most important thing when deciding on an ad campaign is to realize what you want to get from it.

New-school brands are aware that advertising has a place in the world and place should be the main word here. What should adverts truly be used for?

— To make a statement to the world that you are a big brand and so can afford to advertise?

— To show the world the look and feel of your brand in an image?

— To build relationships with magazines and publications?

— To use the ad as part of a bigger strategy so that it is a creative campaign linking to your digital and PR content?

TIP
—

A little secret: if a brand advertises with a publication, they can then leverage off free publicity within the magazine that the reader is not aware has previously been agreed.

If you are doing it just for ego, to show off your brand, then it is to be hoped that your brand has deep pockets. Make sure your advert is placed as part of a strategy that will then be fused with creative thinking and used alongside a plan for the year. A goal you could set is to collaborate with a high-profile photographer or celebrity to endorse the brand so that it creates a talking point for the media to write about the campaign, which in turn raises the profile of the brand by association with the people endorsing it.

Think then about how it can be tied in to a 360° execution – a behind-the-scenes video of the celeb talking about the brand that you can download from the advert or get a longer version of on the website, driving more traffic to the site; a competition that is run in collaboration with a print publication where you can enter, engage with the advert and win the product that is being advertised in a limited edition run of a particular colour. A retailer can be involved in the advert by hosting an evening with the celebrity and also providing window space to play the video in the advert and finally, they can provide all the windows for the logo and promotion of the evening on the advert. The advert can then be tied in with what the vision is, who the face is, why you are using that person, whether they are right for the brand message and the key values to reach out to your target audience.

Surgery successfully used this same process when relaunching Pringle of Scotland back into the marketplace in 2003, before the age of digital came into play. Sophie Dahl, who at the time was very much in the public eye, was to be the face of the brand. By using her image in the campaign we managed to generate over 150 press clippings in the UK alone and featured her on the front cover of five national newspapers. This generated over 1.5 million pounds' worth of free press coverage from one campaign in the UK alone – and it was only shown in print! It was promoted through the Pringle store on Bond Street and Sophie Dahl provided Surgery with an exclusive interview about the campaign – she was also seen modelling in the catwalk show at London Fashion Week wearing a Pringle twin set.

If we were to run this same process today, it would be looking at double that coverage as we would have been getting the same press coverage through online press media and social media hits/shares alike.

LINZIPEDIA: PUBLIC RELATIONS

A free form of advertising that guarantees coverage in publications and online so that the reader buys in to the brand without any money for advertising changing hands. Free PR can be seen on high-fashion pages, shopping pages and features written on individuals/brands. This free form of advertising is a much more believable space and is measured as five times more valuable than any advert placed.

Public relations (PR) is the act of creating a strategy, sending out product, schmoozing the journalists and getting the product to grace the pages of every single relevant publication, worn on your favourite celebs and talked about by all the people in the know so that the product literally walks off the shelves. All for free...

Today, it's a much more saturated space to be able to create the return on investment that a brand is looking for. If you are looking for high-volume coverage and impact, then becoming savvy to the use of advertising and the benefits around it is key.

You may be reading this and thinking that you are not in a space with your brand to be thinking about advertising, or you have realized that for the amount of money needed to spend in this area you would prefer to look at PR as a cheaper way of getting promotion for your brand.

The uses and juices of PR

PR was once the small-brand version of advertising, referred to as being below the line of communication (I have heard it called the poor man's version of marketing). Over the past five years the dynamics have changed and PR is less expensive, yes, yet it provides a much more effective form of advertising; harder to achieve, yet much more valuable to the targeted audience. It is positioned, measured and delivered so that it is targeted to the reader on pages that have been strategically placed for the brand not only through print but now through digital and online blogs. A brand will use an external agency or an in-house PR team to provide them with the strategy and deliverables for their brand.

PR is the most desirable form of media as it is free (you don't pay for your brand to be featured in the publications, you only pay for the time it takes the person or agency to PR your brand).

Free PR is the most believable form of promotion.

HOW DID THIS ALL APPEAR IN THE PUBLICATIONS?

A PR agency or in-house PR team has contacted each publication and sold in the story, person, article or product to enable them to then grace the pages of their magazine for free! Take it from me, working in the industry, nearly everything you read has some sort of PR slant.

This one statement should explain to you the value of an advert versus the value of PR. How many times do you open up a magazine, see a bus go by or a taxi, and ignore the advert that is being presented to you? When you open up a publication and see the must-have item of the season that is either being sported by Kate Moss or another of your favourite celebrities, or in a list of the 10 most wanted items that season, do you want to run out and buy it?

If you are shouting out "yes, of course" then you are not alone!

Let me tell you that an advert in a magazine will have cost anything upwards of three to tens of thousands of pounds per page and so many times we find the reader has turned the page without a second glance – even got annoyed that there are too many adverts at the front of the magazine when they only want to read the content. When you are paying a PR agency or an in-house PR team anything from £20,000 a year upwards whilst receiving over a million pounds' worth of free publicity a season, is the cost of PR relatively cheap or expensive?

What you don't realize is that the whole magazine is an advert for brands, quite simply some are paid for through adverts that you can see and the others are hidden in the content and paid for through the use of PR. You may choose to advertise and PR your brand. However, by far the most powerful and effective way of promoting and driving your brand forward is to incorporate it all into a 360° communications strategy.

THE 360° TOUCHPOINTS APPROACH TO FULL COMMUNICATION

Both PR and advertising agencies have developed and evolved their services since the Internet was launched, with both parties realizing that in order to create the deliverables required by medium/large-size brands and to stay ahead of the game, they have to provide a wider offering to be more effective in supporting a brand's growth.

A 360° approach to a full communication strategy looks at every area of your business geared to determining and then communicating your key message and brand objectives for the business. It provides a full communication service and brand development strategy so that the brand can grow using all the relevant touchpoints to enable you to communicate with your end consumer in a multi-faceted approach.

Some ad agencies saw the change of direction with advertising and bought in to smaller PR agencies so that they could offer the 360° approach; other agencies like mine created new divisions and services to be able to service a variety of clients all under one roof.

Why use the full 360° approach?

At Surgery we incorporate touchpoints to form the structure of a 360° communication strategy so that it can be tailored to a brand in order to define the key messages to their specific target audience. Being able to communicate, develop and build brands enables the brand to drive forward, which takes them to a place that far outreaches the realms of traditional standalone PR.

LINZIPEDIA: TOUCHPOINTS

A touchpoint is a point that links five points to create a perfect circle. Taking one big idea, it is communicated through the five touchpoints: traditional PR (print and digital), social media and digital engagement, brand partnerships/collaborations, retail engagement, experiential events in a 360° approach to make the circle complete. Any individual use of these touchpoints will be less than the sum of the parts that make up the whole.

A touch on points

With any brand we encourage engagement of the five key touchpoints that create the 360° communication platform to ensure we talk to the end consumer through a multi-platform approach – traditional PR (print and digital), social media and digital engagement, brand partnerships/collaborations, retail engagement, experiential events.

Using any touchpoint on its own minimizes your reach, whereas using all five touchpoints together ensures that you will see the benefits of a multiplier effect. This means you are using not just one channel but multiple channels to engage your end consumer, gaining guaranteed maximum reach in a way that one channel could miss.

The 360° approach to engaging with your customer has to encompass the brand design, product creation and marketing tools necessary to action any idea you have. These can be created by using freelance designers; one large creative agency that can action all the different areas or a number of smaller creative agencies that specialize in each area you need. There is no right or wrong way to achieve your result, it just comes down to choice and budget allocated.

Do you find yourself asking...

"How am I going to manage to promote my own brand?"
"Is promotion very expensive and can I do it myself?"

You are at present sitting in a place of unknowns, not sure what to do or how to do it. Know that, by the time you have finished reading this book, all that should have changed. You will have been given all the knowledge you need to really get going with building and elevating you brand.

FIVE SIMPLE STEPS ARE OUTLINED FOR YOU THROUGHOUT THIS BOOK

You can choose to read them and use the knowledge to engage with agencies that can create the content and implement it for you, or you can implement the steps for yourself. You will know what feels right to you once you have started to read and understand how each step works, and how they are joined together to create, engage and elevate your brand...

@LINZI_BOYD

63

PART 02

THE FIVE STEPS TO STAND-OUT BRAND SUCCESS

—

JOINING
THE DOTS...

—

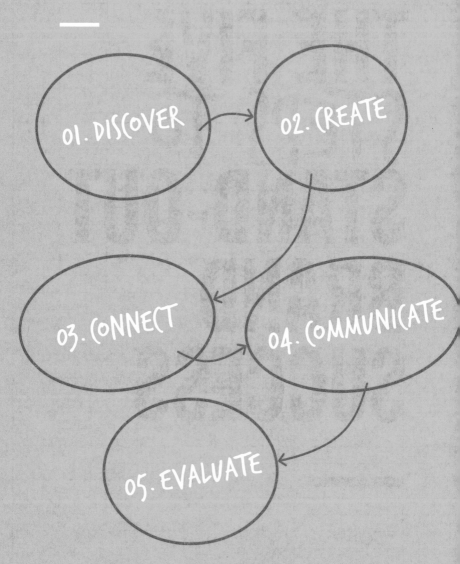

01. DISCOVER

02. CREATE

03. CONNECT

04. COMMUNICATE

05. EVALUATE

You are now ready to start the process: it is time for you to allow your creative seed to grow.

THIS PROCESS IS ALL ABOUT...

—

01 Where you are now
02 Where you want to be
03 How to get there

Achieve the goals that you set out to maximize
your exposure

Imagine that the only thing ever really holding you back is you; driving it, promoting it, living and breathing it, making it and sometimes faking it whilst always dressing it up for success. You and your team are the brand and you must act like the brand. It does not matter if you have one person or 2000 people working on your brand – you have to work on your brand and not in your brand.

Be your brand, live your brand, own your brand
and when you are not sure, make it up

Make sure that you have a powerful mindset and know what you have set out to say. Own your space. If you don't believe that you are the number 1 brand in your field then how will you convince anyone else of this?

Here we set out the five-step sequence that you need. It will enable you to own your space and take your rightful place in your market. Learn to understand that underneath everything lie the words that you are saying and how you deliver these to the outside world is as important as the product you have. Once you have established yourself with the mindset of a stand-out big brand and used the five steps, you will never have thoughts counter to this again.

Each step is made up of a series of "dots" that you can follow through in sequence. You will be given the tools to promote your brand through the different communication platforms that are freely available to you. By joining these dots you will be sure to stand out from the crowd, create a buzz around your brand and collaborate with the best of the best in your field. I look forward to seeing it, reading about it, having celebrities using it, wearing it, literally bumping into it everywhere!

STEP 01 #DISCOVER

DISCOVER YOUR BRAND VALUES AND KEY MESSAGE, YOUR POSITIONING IN THE MARKET, WHO YOU ARE TALKING TO AND WHY THEY WILL LISTEN

—

STEP 02 #CREATE

CREATE YOUR PRODUCT LINES/SERVICES AND YOUR TOOLKIT TO SPREAD AWARENESS OF THEM

—

STEP 03 #CONNECT

DISTRIBUTE YOUR PRODUCT/SERVICE INTO THE MARKETPLACE

—

STEP 04 #COMMUNICATE

USE THE FIVE "TOUCHPOINTS" TO CREATE YOUR VOICE

—

STEP 05 #EVALUATE

KNOW WHEN YOUR BRAND HAS ACHIEVED STAND-OUT STATUS BY SETTING AND MEASURING YOUR KPI AND ROI

—

SHALL WE MOVE ON? LET THE PROCESS BEGIN...

———

CHAPTER 04:
STEP ONE #DISCOVER

—

THE TRUE ESSENCE OF YOUR BRAND

—

Enter into the Discovery Phase...

This is the most vital stage for any brand. It enables you to discover the key message that is sitting underneath your brand and the core values that will set its blueprint moving forwards. It will provide you with the foundation to work from with the next four steps provided in this book.

By the end of this chapter my goal is for you to have a clear understanding of what the intention is behind your brand, how you are positioned to be seen by the world, who you are talking to so that you can engage with your audience and what your point of difference is so that you stand out from the crowd. It should allow you to move on with confidence, knowing that you have laid down solid foundations for the base of your house, and your brand will be able to hold a strong position in its marketplace once the house is built. Done haphazardly or glossed over, it will affect the remaining four steps as you attempt to build a roof without having the walls in place first.

The discover phase is vital to the whole brand. Without doing it, you may as well build a car without the engine.

LET THE DOT-TO-DOT BEGIN. DISCOVER YOUR BRAND

You will find that you have to connect with your brand, or in some cases reconnect with your brand, and the reason you created your brand in the first place. You may already have some ideas about what your brand means to you but have not yet explored them in depth. Maybe you've had your business for a number of years and have not been seeing success, so you need to reconnect with your brand values in order to re-engage with your target audience. Perhaps you carried out a brand audit in the past, but have since found that it does not actually match your brand message and values. In truth it's time to rediscover the core/true essence of your brand.

LINZIPEDIA: BRAND AUDIT

This is an assessment of where your brand is at the moment, looking at how well you know your own brand and how well other people know it. The brand famous audit will look at your mission, vision, values, awareness and desirability using the five key principles written about in this book to provide the results.

The discover phase defines the DNA of your brand and, if done correctly, can be incorporated into the vision of your next three-year plan. It will deliver you a way to apply the information through your visual and verbal language which comes in the form of branding, website, videos, creative look and feel through to product lines and communication plan. It really does impact on everything that you do in moving forward from this point.

The best way to work through the discover phase is to gather the key people from your business and work together on answering the following action points given within each dot. If you each answer the questions and then compare notes, it will enable you to come up with the true answers as to where your brand values lie. If you are still small and haven't these people inside the business, then reach out to your friends/family.

Can I make a suggestion? Go away for the day, turn off the computers, engage with your colleagues, sit in a space that is creative and inviting, buy yourselves a crisp clean notepad and pen (I love nothing more) and engage with the project at hand.

PLAY THE DISCOVER DOT-TO-DOT GAME

INSTRUCTIONS

—

Read the dot, then play the game. Work your way through each chapter.

GETTING UNDERNEATH YOUR BRAND

—

GAME 01

WHAT IS YOUR BRAND AND WHAT IS IT NOT?

KEY MESSAGE AND CORE VALUES

—

GAME 02

WHAT MAKES YOUR BRAND YOUR BRAND?

THE PERSONALITY

—

GAME 03

GIVE YOUR BRAND A PERSONALITY

DOT 07

JUDGING YOUR BRAND

—

GAME 07
FOCUS ON THE APPEARANCE OF THE BRAND

DOT 06

TARGETS AND GOALS

—

GAME 06
WHO ARE YOU TALKING TO, AND ARE THEY LISTENING?

DOT 05

UNDERSTANDING NEEDS AND HABITS

—

GAME 05A/B
DEFINE NEEDS OR HABITS

DOT 04

TARGET AUDIENCE

—

GAME 04
TALKING/LISTENING?

@LINZI_BOYD

GETTING UNDERNEATH
YOUR BRAND
—

Who am I and who am I not?

This is an interesting and thought-provoking question to ask when working with a brand in a workshop environment. This dot is a great one to get you and your team excited. It gets you clear on what you want to be known for so that when you are creating your branding, visuals and product it is very simple to brief someone in and be precise on what you are and what you are not.

I witness a lot of passion around what people say their brand is not and what they believe their brand could be in the future! You may also find some conflict of opinions and this is why it is great to work in a group with your team members to get underneath how everybody sees the "personality" of your brand. It very much shapes and defines where you want your brand perception to be within the market.

GAMES OR
NOTE PAPER
IN THE BACK

GAME 01
WHAT IS YOUR BRAND AND WHAT IS IT NOT?

—

Answer the following questions in four columns:

WHAT IS YOUR BRAND TODAY?

WHAT IS YOUR BRAND NOT TODAY?

WHAT COULD YOUR BRAND BE IN THE FUTURE?

WHAT IS STOPPING YOU FROM GETTING THERE?

CREATING YOUR KEY
MESSAGE AND CORE VALUES

Many people fail to understand the meaning of the word values. When it comes to brand values it's about understanding why you do what you do, what the brand truly stands for, providing your brand with its personality and the reasons for bringing the brand into being in the first place. If you set up the business to simply earn money, with no soul or greater purpose or meaning, then the business will struggle. When you get to grips with your highest value and make everything you do align with that highest value, then you are more likely to succeed in business.

The next problem is when the people you have working in your business don't know what the brand values are – how can they work towards these values if they are not clear on what they are? Your key message and core values are absolutely crucial to making your business work and your brand stand out. What I have always found confusing is when a company defines their brand values and then goes to market with an unfinished job or they put them in the drawer to gather dust without integrating them into everything they do. Unless you know who you are and what you are trying to say, how are you or your team supposed to engage your customer in a conversation let alone be able to sell to them?

Your key message and core values, as determined in your brand audit, need to run across everything that you:

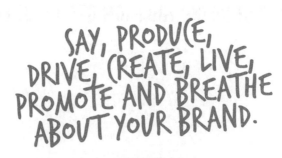

SAY, PRODUCE, DRIVE, CREATE, LIVE, PROMOTE AND BREATHE ABOUT YOUR BRAND.

GAME 02
WHAT MAKES YOUR BRAND YOUR BRAND?

___

An easy place to start is by using words only:

WHAT ARE THE KEY WORDS/MESSAGE WHEN TALKING ABOUT YOUR BRAND?

Use words and short bullet-point sentences – no long sentences required, as you will not want to read back over an essay. Keep it short and very much to the point.

#DISCOVER

FORMING THE PERSONALITY OF YOUR BRAND

You should now find that you are starting to give your brand a personality and an emotional energy that you can then use throughout all areas of your business. Does the way you deliver everything leave people feeling the way you want it to? If not, then change how you do things so that it does.

Think about the environment that people will enter into when they start working with you. Does the way your office looks reflect how people will feel? Is your branding reflective of this in terms of your messaging, the way you deliver pitches, how your team engages not only with clients but also with each other?

Once your brand starts to come alive in this way, you can begin to delve deeper. What is your point of difference? You may have, for example, outstanding service but what does that really mean? It's time to go deeper into this area and define what it is that makes you provide those outstanding services. Are you a people company? Is your price exceptional in relation to the service you provide? It's not enough to say "outstanding service". Be specific, it's time to go that little bit further!

❝ ❞
—

Mike Harris, the founder of Egg and first direct, calls this your iconic pitch. It's the one phrase you can deliver so that people know exactly what you are and what you are offering.

GAME 03
GIVE YOUR BRAND
A PERSONALITY

—

WHAT DO YOU WANT YOUR BRAND
TO BE KNOWN FOR?

This has to reflect on the true essence of what lies within your passion. You will know when you have it as it will "fit".

HOW DO YOU WANT TO LEAVE PEOPLE FEELING
EACH AND EVERY TIME THEY ENGAGE WITH
YOUR BRAND?

Midas is known for turning celebrities into brands and creating product growth for entrepreneurial leaders. We leave them feeling energized for change.

When you meet someone new, engage in a conversation, create a sale, deliver a sale, have a phone conversation, work with a client – any time you have any connection with your customer – how do you want to leave them feeling?

LB SUGGESTS

—

If you are struggling with who you are and what you want to be known for, ask potential new clients how you have left them feeling after a meeting with them. Also look to interview past clients – people that you have provided a service to – so that they can tell you what they got from the experience with you and your brand.

#DISCOVER

DEFINING YOUR TARGET AUDIENCE

—

You might be delivering a product that offers outstanding quality at an affordable price with groundbreaking results; think about the thread that truly makes you different and stand out, then dig deeper to find out what your brand's unique qualities are.

If you don't know what your core message is, how are you supposed to be able to tell your potential clients? How are the people that work for you going to be in a position to relay that message in their daily actions? How are you supposed to have consistency in everything you do? And finally, is your core message aligned with your highest value?

Ask yourself whether you have ever launched, or are about to launch, a product without fully understanding who that product is for (or you may have thought you knew your target audience but got it completely wrong!).

Have you ever believed that you were talking to your audience through the appropriate communication channels, i.e. an advert, Facebook or magazine article, and then realized (after the launch) that you needed to pick up on the campaign because your audience don't actually follow that channel of communication?

Would you like to work with celebrity or ambassador partnerships but are unclear as to why you would do that or even which celebrity is right for your business? (More on this later...)

Your target audience is the thing that connects you with your end consumer; if you define this, it will enable you to know who you are speaking to and drive sales to your product. I wonder whether you are aware that without truly defining who your audience is and extracting the information from your core message and values that your audience needs to know, you can never be sure that your product is connecting with the end consumer to enable the product to sell off the shelves.

The simplest way to define your target audience is by asking direct questions that will form a picture of the person you are speaking to.

GAME 04
WHO ARE YOU TALKING TO, AND ARE THEY LISTENING?

—

If you want to find out about a person or business, you could ask the following questions.

WHAT IS YOUR TARGET AUDIENCE DEMOGRAPHIC?

— How old are they? Finding out their age provides the sweet spot of your target audience, so you can then eliminate older and younger from the equation.

— What are they influenced by? For example, what do they read, are they heavily into online activity and if so of which form – social media or online publications? Where do they shop, what do they buy? Blogs, tweets, etc. will all be defined by their age.

— What income bracket are they in – low, middle or high – and define what the 53 brackets are.

WHAT IS THE SIZE OF THE MARKET?

— Is your primary base your home town and then second and third two other places in the world?

IF YOUR COMPANY IS BUSINESS TO BUSINESS THEN YOU CAN ALSO DEFINE

— The size of their business (startup, early growth, etc.).

— What type of business you are speaking to (be specific) – is there a primary target and then a secondary target?

THE DOCTOR OF ALTERNATIVE HEALTH

—

I recently worked with a doctor in the <u>discover phase</u> who wanted to look at her brand vision and values. She was working in a holistic health environment with a method that took away the need for invasive western medicine. When running a workshop with her we explored who she was speaking to – both consumers and professionals – and it was interesting to see who her target audience was and their varying demographics.

It came about that she was speaking to three types of people:

The Converted
Middle market, upper in income from about £30,000 and above. They are interested in alternative therapies and like to read books on holistic health, environmental issues, popular science and alternative health by authors such as Deepak Choprah and Eckhart Toll. They are in pursuit of alternative medicine and ways to heal themselves. They use the Internet regularly to research new things available and regularly shop online. They have an open mind and crave new experiences.

The Unconverted (this is the secondary audience)
Those who only stick to the conventional way because they don't know any different; aged 18–30. They are open minded and would gladly look into something new if they were presented with it. They would be frustrated by conventional medicine and are running out of options. Starting out in employment, they are earning £15,000–£25,000. They read most of their articles or features online and listen to their friends/communities.

The Skeptic
Working as a practitioner or within the medical profession. They are open to alternative ways of treating a patient but are a lot harder to convert. They have questions yet are curious and willing to look at change if presented with the scientific evidence behind it. They use the Internet for research and also read magazines, trade publications and attend seminars. They earn an income of £40,000 upwards.

Her primary market was the UK; however, America was a secondary target for its open-minded attitude and Europe third.

Consider, now, the value of understanding your target audience in this way. What could you do differently?

You will see from the above that an older person's profile will be very different from a younger person's profile. These days, both will go online for information but the amount they use it and what they use will be very different.

Once you are clear on these two aspects, you then need to look deeper into who you are talking to. Where they work, shop, live and what they drive all define if the person is a low, middle or high earner. You may be talking to a particular age group, and yet someone who is still at college in Oxford, drives a mini and dresses head to toe in Jack Wills has a very clear differentiation from someone of the same age group who lives in the East End of London, is a runner on a film set and travels around on the tube.

DO YOU SEE THE PICTURE FORMING? ARE YOU CREATING YOUR PEOPLE YET?

By drawing up a full picture of your target audience's needs, you will define who you are going to speak to, how you will speak to them, why you will speak to them and what information you will provide them with so that you know you are connecting with them through the appropriate channels in a way that meets with their needs and desires.

Everything you produce will be focused towards that target audience and, if you then want to create another new product line, you should understand that the same process is required in order to achieve a new audience or sell to the same audience in a different way. I often work with brands that speak to more than one target audience. The difference between success and failure in this case lies in those that have clearly defined who they are speaking to and which channel they will use to communicate with them. This means that they will not cross-contaminate products or messages that self-sabotage their existing customer base in order to create a new one.

#DISCOVER

UNDERSTANDING YOUR CUSTOMERS' NEEDS OR HABITS

Now you have looked at who you are speaking to, have a think about why you want to speak to them and whether or not there are any particular needs or habits in that market group that create a desire for them to buy in to your brand and not those of your competitors.

Any successful brand, as far as I am aware, normally acts in one of two ways when looking to create their product line – in terms of speaking to their target audience:

01   They look to provide their target market with a brand that creates either a new need/habit or

02   They build on and nurture an existing need/habit.

Either way, they engage with what the customer really wants without them even realizing that they have a desire for it yet!

NEEDS AND HABITS

A need occurs when a customer looks at your product and thinks, "I need that" or comparatively, "I don't need that". One buys, the other doesn't. A habit is something that is done repetitively on a consistent basis. A brand that taps into that process and makes life easier for the consumer will create an "I need that" process which leads to a purchase. For instance, you check emails every day and all of a sudden you can check them on a new phone.

A great example of attempting to create a new "need" in the marketplace was the spork – a hybrid product merging a fork and a spoon. I believe the target audience is children, fast food restaurants, backpackers and perhaps a picnic or two. The media successfully received it into the marketplace; however, I am unaware whether sales matched up to the media attention. The question arises, has the spork created a habit for people to move away from the fork and spoon concept? In some areas, such as picnics and fast food, it may lead to a preference for the consumer. Most likely, people failed to see a need for the product when forks and spoons have served us so well for many years; although they enjoyed the gimmick in store, they would not buy in to the end product.

A new habit was created by Apple who, as we know, provided the consumer with the tablet and the iPhone – creating a generation of touchscreen swiping that had never been seen before. Apple are the pioneers of delivering new habits, and it is ever more difficult to emulate this within a market sector. To change a person's habit from what they know and are used to and get them to use something completely new is a challenge that most brands face. There are still older generations today that are not tech savvy and have only just got the hang of mobile phones and computers, never mind tablets and iPhones. For the younger generations, however, you are building on existing habits and behaviours that will have been formed as part of their memory pattern since they have been surrounded by such gadgets since birth. I do wonder what will be perceived as a new need or habit for them.

Building on an existing need is something that we did with our shoes, noticing a gap in the market for fashion-related trainers when at the time there were only sports-related ones, thus paving the way to fill a need that was ready for the taking.

I have personally always found this an easier area to work in, as you are not in a space of changing the mindset of someone's habits or providing them with a new need, just shifting their state of play into a natural next step transition of where they could/would organically go.

DEFINE YOUR CUSTOMERS' NEEDS OR HABITS

—

01 WHAT IS THE NEED OR HABIT THAT YOU ARE TRYING TO PROVIDE YOUR CUSTOMERS WITH THAT MAKES YOUR BRAND DIFFERENT FROM YOUR COMPETITORS' BRANDS?

02 ARE YOU PROVIDING THEM WITH A NEW NEED/HABIT OR ARE YOU SPEAKING TO AN EXISTING NEED/HABIT?

Now, you know who your customers are and what their needs/habits are that would enable them to look at buying into your brand. Think about who your competitors are that you believe sit in the marketplace already.

I often hear people say that their brand/product offering is so unique that they do not feel they have competitors, or others that feel they have too many to list. Think about the space that you want to own and who sits there at the moment. Where do they sell their product? How does their website look? What is their tone of voice and how do they position themselves to their customers? I would even go one step further and play a game where you assess what the need or habit is that they are providing to their customer and try to draw a picture of who their target audience is.

GAME 05B
DEFINE YOUR COMPETITORS CUSTOMERS' NEEDS OR HABITS

—

01 WRITE DOWN THE TOP THREE COMPETITOR BRANDS IN YOUR MARKET SECTOR.

02 WHO DO YOU FEEL IS THEIR TARGET AUDIENCE?

03 WHAT DO YOU SEE AS THEIR STRENGTHS AND WEAKNESSES?

04 WHAT IS THE NEED/HABIT THAT THEY ARE PROVIDING TO THEIR CUSTOMERS?

You must always remember that this is a game that you are playing and you will always play to win; however, ultimately you will play it just for the love of it. There is no better way to work on your business than to treat it as a game. It is the thing that will get you out of bed in the morning and keep you motivated throughout the day. You are the master of your own destiny and must set your targets to meet your goals so that they are achievable and slightly unreachable. Remember, start to walk. There will be no one that can hold you back, except yourself. Believe that you can take the biggest slice of the pie and you will take ownership of your rightful place within your market.

Mike Harris, the author of *Find Your Lightbulb* (findyour lightbulb.com) and founder of Egg and first direct, said to me: "Take risks that won't leave you in the ditch." That, for me, says it all... Don't be scared to reach for the unreachable; however, don't do it to the extent of losing your business or your life.

It's just a game ... play full out.

#DISCOVER

SETTING YOUR TARGETS AND GOALS

When setting your goals, look back at the brand values and core message and use these to underpin what targets you would like to set and the goals you ultimately want to meet.

Where you are today, where you want to be and the obstacles that are holding you back should form the basis of the goals and objectives for your strategy whilst always having the core message and brand values underlying everything that you create around your brand. Your target audience can expand and change, but the essence of your brand will always stay the same.

You must set goals that are achievable, which increase the awareness of your brand, enable you to take a big portion of your chosen market, increase your turnover and deliver great results whilst keeping you and your brand in the public eye.

Think about the most important things that will take you to #brandfamous status. You are about to play the game and gain the results and momentum that you have always known you could get but were unsure how to achieve. What is needed to play your game? What is needed to realize your true potential and execute your product, ideas and core proposition so that the information you generate from the workbook suits your plan and is executed to drive your brand forward?

To create a stand-out status requires everything that you produce to clearly speak one key message with a succinct look, set against everything you produce. How can you expect your target audience to listen to you if your message is not spread across everything that you write, produce, say and do?

GAME 06

WHO ARE YOU TALKING TO, AND ARE THEY LISTENING?

List below your big-thinking vision for your brand (there should be no more than three to five items).

List the small steps to get you there

BIG THINKING

SMALL STEPS

The last big dot to prepare you for the game ahead

You may be wondering how the use of your brand values as an objective to set goals can deliver future results to your business. Who you are, and what your key message is, are at the core of everything that you create and deliver to your consumer. One of your goals has to be to incorporate your key message and brand values so that they are present in everything that you produce. This way you have one clear message running through everything that you do.

If your company is transformational, exciting and forward thinking then the look and feel of your business and everything you produce, and/or the services you provide, must scream out these words and speak your language.

LB SUGGESTS

Can I ask you to leave people feeling like they have been transformed, that they have seen something new and are left feeling excited by their transformation? Your first objective should be to use key words from your brand values to demonstrate this, and the message that you have is the product/service you will provide to your customer.

#DISCOVER

JUDGING YOUR BRAND BY ITS COVER

Why do you find so many people talking about how things look, surely having an outstanding product/service is enough? We live in a world where we are moved by looks first and function second. People are driven by the pretty bow that is on the box and the packaging. Think back to the last time you bought a stand-out product. How was the packaging? Did this draw you in as much as, if not more than, the product that you found hidden inside the box?

Do you think that everyone buys in to an Apple Mac product only because of its functionality outweighing everything else in the marketplace? If you ask a person such as myself, who owns more than one Apple Mac product, you will probably find most of them say that they have bought in to the beauty and aesthetics of each design. We all know what the iPhone, iPad and MacBook Air can do, but if they didn't look the way they do, would they have been market leaders? The products certainly look great, and don't you find that you feel you have bought something worth having when the packaging is as great as the product.

When you are putting together the branding for your business, always stretch yourself that little bit further, think about your end consumer and how they will feel when they buy in to what you are offering, know that we are all human and everyone likes to be left feeling special. I always like to think of my services as a present, and the feeling you get when you receive a gift is something that I like to replicate when providing someone with any information from my company.

THINK ABOUT YOUR END CUSTOMER

FOCUS ON THE APPEARANCE OF YOUR BRAND

—

WRITE OUT A LIST OF THE AREAS WHERE YOU CAN INCORPORATE YOUR KEY MESSAGE AND CORE VALUES IN PLACES THAT YOUR END USER WILL ENGAGE WITH IT.

Examples of engaging places within your work:

Entrance to your office: Graphic message on the wall

Office space: Engaging colours, furniture

Meeting room: Brochures, pencils, tea set

Website: Creative website/e-commerce site attached

Know your space in the marketplace and own it
If your core message is technical equipment that is high performing and driven, then produce packaging that speaks to your customer. Think about the colours and textures of materials, and incorporate your vision into your brand and its packaging.

If you want to set up a yoga retreat in Ibiza that is targeting yummy mummies bringing along their kids, then know that these women are already buying in to the luxury sector and would not buy in to your brand if it does not scream out high quality whilst also speaking to the kids as a byproduct.

You should have a tick list that is all run from your brand guidelines. Everything that you say should be mirrored across everything that you do, so you have a clear message that speaks to your end consumer.

FROM PAIN TO
PEAK PERFORMANCE

———

I was recently working with a unique business that has an education system using a method that enables people to get out of pain and into peak performance quickly (sometimes within three minutes). They teach this method to osteopaths, physios, PTs and chiropractors so that they can then incorporate the method into their practices and produce groundbreaking results with their clients.

They are still in the build stage with their business – it's been trading for four years – and have an understanding of who they are and where they want to be positioned. They have had the same branding and website for the last four years. They have a very directional and transformational business, but this was not reflected in any of the material that their end consumer was seeing.

I worked with them in the discover phase to help them get underneath the passion of the brand. When I started working with this company the owner was "quite attached" to the appearance that he had used for four years, and understandably did not want to lose his existing identity. However, we set about presenting the workshop information to our in-house graphic team to create the branding that could lend itself to everything that they needed to produce. Obviously the logo and website, but we also showed them a whole presentation of how it could go on videos, images, clothes and then even more exciting creative consumer products that could both be used with his students and sold through retail stores, both off- and online to create a whole new revenue stream.

When we presented him with his "transformational looking brand", he went on to change everything within his company over the next six months and has now moved his company on more in this period of time in terms of look and feel, creating product lines, developing videos and websites and opening up new territories in key cities around the world to teach his method. He told us, when comparing his new branding with his old branding (which he was heavily attached to), that he couldn't believe how "young" it looked and that he now felt like the brand had finally grown up.

" "

—

Design is not just what it looks like and feels like. Design is how it works.

Steve Jobs
Co-founder and former CEO of Apple Inc.

The discover phase has been about providing the people that make the growth of your business possible, a bigger picture into your world. Everyone should now have clear guidelines on where you are and what you stand for, and more importantly what you are not and where you will never be. Once you have this information, you will be able to produce your product so that it speaks to your target audience and write your communication strategy so that you go to market through the correct distribution channel with a mindset that will allow your customer to understand the values of your business.

DISCOVER PHASE → IDEA
= CREATE

— Carry your brand message.

— Support your vision and values for the brand.

— Speak directly to your target audience in a language they understand.

— Infiltrate the areas of communication and technology that your target audience engages with.

QUICK PEEK CHEAT SHEET

—

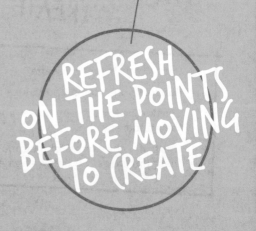

REFRESH ON THE POINTS BEFORE MOVING TO CREATE

01 GETTING UNDERNEATH YOUR BRAND
WHAT IS YOUR BRAND AND WHAT IS IT NOT?

---

02 CREATING YOUR KEY MESSAGES AND CORE VALUES
WHAT MAKES YOUR BRAND YOUR BRAND?

---

03 FORMING THE PERSONALITY OF YOUR BRAND
GIVE YOUR BRAND A PERSONALITY

---

04 DEFINING YOUR TARGET AUDIENCE
WHO ARE YOU TALKING TO AND ARE THEY LISTENING?

---

05 UNDERSTANDING YOUR CUSTOMERS' NEEDS OR HABITS
CREATE OR BUILD A NEED/HABIT

---

06 SETTING YOUR TARGETS AND GOALS
TAKE SMALL STEPS TO BIG THINKING

---

07 JUDGING YOUR BRAND BY ITS COVER
FOCUS ON THE APPEARANCE OF YOUR BRAND

Enter your information at the school of brand fame to gain more insight and also a game summary.
www.brandfamous.com/schoolofbrandfame

CHAPTER 05:
STEP TWO #CREATE

YOUR PRODUCT VISION

Enter into the Create Phase...

Creation is the key to producing stand-out product lines and services; providing your brand with a voice that speaks the passion of the brand. The create section is designed to give you greater insight into how a PRODUCT PLAN could look for you and your business. It was written to provide you with an understanding of the importance of creating the right product for your brand, and to open you up to the possibility that your brand could carry multiple product line categories rather than the usual one or two. In the product vision map provided in this chapter, you will be able to plot out your product plan to show the different types of product you will create, and to make it easier for you I will walk you through the different types of product category accessible to any marketplace. It provides you with an opportunity to look at manufacturing options and see what you have available and why this is so important when producing your brand.

LET THE DOT-TO-DOT BEGIN. CREATE YOUR BRAND

Before entering into the product vision and creation section, I invite you to look at the tools that are needed in order to create awareness around the products that you decide to sell. As mentioned above, there are two key categories required in order to get your business running like a well-oiled machine:

1. TOOLKIT CREATION
2. PRODUCT/SERVICE CREATION

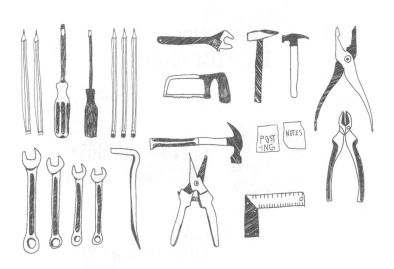

PLAY THE CREATE
DOT-TO-DOT GAME

—

INSTRUCTIONS

—

Read the dot, then play the game. Work your way through each chapter.

**WORKING OUT WHERE
YOU ARE TODAY
WITH YOUR PRODUCT/
SERVICE**

—

GAME 01
**CREATE YOUR
ESSENTIAL TOOLKIT**

**GETTING THE MOST
FROM YOUR TOOLKIT**

—

GAME 02
**CREATE YOUR OWN
BESPOKE TOOLKIT**

SAMPLING YOUR
PRODUCT
—

GAME 06
ASSESS AND ROAD TEST
YOUR PRODUCT

DEFINING WHERE BEST
TO PRODUCE YOUR
PRODUCT
—

GAME 05
WHERE TO PRODUCE
THE PRODUCT

WORKING OUT YOUR
PRODUCT OPTIONS
—

GAME 04
CREATE YOUR PRODUCT
VISION PYRAMID

CREATING PRODUCTS AND SERVICES
WITH ONE BUSINESS MODEL
—

GAME 03
CHART YOUR CURRENT
PRODUCT/SERVICE

#CREATE

CREATING THE TOOLKIT FOR YOUR BRAND

Why on earth do I need a toolkit in my business?
It's simple really, one feeds off the other. Toolkit creation is essential in order to sell your product line and without it there is very little point in having any product to sell. And no, I am not talking about tools such as a hammer or a screwdriver although it is pretty much the same philosophy – you would not use a screwdriver where a hammer is required and you would not drill something into a wall with a pencil.

Every business requires an essential toolkit in order for it to run efficiently and effectively, so that product can sell and be promoted through the correct channels. Your business should be exactly the same. Every business that Surgery works with is presented with a "toolkit requirement sheet" that is used to work out whether each tool is produced and created to a certain standard and is able to deliver on what is required from it. Why? So that the toolkit can be used as a tool to create the awareness that is needed to drive traffic/sales to the business.

LINZIPEDIA: TOOLKIT

A toolkit is a set of promotional material needed in any business in order to promote your brand efficiently and effectively. It is called a toolkit as they are essential tools for any business.

Each business has an essential set of tools that is STANDARD to any business and a BESPOKE set that is required for that particular type of business. I cannot stress how important it is that every brand creates the essential toolkit so that you are able to promote your product through the correct channels and ultimately get a high return on your investment.

You will of course want to individualize your toolkit so that it is bespoke to your business; however, if you first have the basics that I have listed below then your business will run efficiently without concern.

CREATE YOUR ESSENTIAL TOOLKIT

—

Without these essential tools you have no way of communicating your product out to the world in today's business environment.

WHAT FORMS THE BASIS OF AN ESSENTIAL TOOLKIT? TICK WHICH ONES YOU HAVE:

WEBSITE ○

VIRAL VIDEOS ○

PROMOTIONAL VIDEOS FROM EVENTS ○

E-SHOTS – MINI PRESS RELEASES PROMOTING ONE PRODUCT ○

SALES BROCHURE ○

LOOK BOOK – IMAGERY OF PRODUCT ○

BIOGRAPHY OF OWNER/CEO ○

HEAD SHOT OF OWNER/CEO ○

PRESS RELEASE OUTLINING MULTIPLE PRODUCT LAUNCH ○

FLAT SHOT IMAGERY TO USE ONLINE ○

THE 06 COMMON MISTAKES PEOPLE MAKE WHEN NOT CREATING A TOOLKIT

---

01 NOT HAVING ANYWHERE TO SHOWCASE WHAT YOU DO

Without a toolkit, people find they have nowhere to showcase any past work, future events and all the rich content you produce in your day-to-day running of the business. A website is your window to the world and forms part of your toolkit.

02 NOT HAVING A SALES BROCHURE

There are no sales brochures attached to the services so when a new customer asks them what they do, there is nothing to support it or send out.

03 NOT USING VIDEO TO PROMOTE YOUR PRODUCT/SERVICE

We are living in a digital age; the quickest way to engage your customer is through video, yet most people would regard this as too new age and expensive to even consider.

04 NOT HAVING IMAGERY TO SUPPORT YOUR PRODUCT/SERVICE

There are no images of the product so when a new customer or a journalist wants to write about the product line, there is nothing to send.

05 MISMATCHED BRANDING AND MESSAGING

All the branding has been created so that nothing is coherent with anything else; when you send something out it does not create the same message.

06 NOT THINKING ABOUT YOURSELF AS A TOOL

Try to remember that people talking and writing about your brand like to have as much information about the person behind the brand – by making sure that the imagery is high quality and well shot so that people are able to use the shot and do not have to reshoot which costs money and takes time.

#CREATE

GETTING THE MOST FROM YOUR TOOLKIT

One thing you must remember when creating your toolkit is that everything must be linked to your brand DNA that you have already created above in the discover phase. It must all have the same look and feel and tone of voice and be able to look like it has come from one stable. Once you do this, you stand in a space of authority knowing who you are, what you stand for and who you are speaking to so that your customer will listen. When you create your toolkit along the same lines, you will be able to see clearly which tools you require to speak to your target audience so that they will actually watch, listen and leave wanting more.

In the past you have probably created videos or produced sales content with no thought about who you are speaking to or for what reason. You have just known that you should be doing something since everyone else is. You must know why you are producing the video and what you want it to do for you.

Won't it be a relief to be clear on the purpose for creating your content so you know exactly what it is for and who is going to engage with it? Most importantly, it will actually connect and engage with people to create a ripple effect so they truly buy in to your brand and dare I say it become loyal customers.

You will also start to get a picture of which product lines you want to produce to create hype around your brand so as to engage your customer, ensuring your product literally flies off the shelves or your service is in high demand.

You have now seen your essential tools list so you can create your essential toolkit. That is not to say that it all has to be designed identically. You can have an essential kit and a bespoke model depending on what you want to create. The essential kit outlines what is needed to create the basic package so that you are able to sell and market your product. The bespoke kit provides you with a more creative individual approach to engage with your customer in a unique and directional way that sets you apart from your competitors.

Within this space we are always looking at different ways to grab a new client's attention so that they want to work with either the agency or a brand.

CREATE YOUR OWN BESPOKE TOOLKIT

Think of three creative ways that you can create your bespoke toolkit and engage with your customer in a way that makes you unique and stand out.

IDEA ONE

IDEA TWO

IDEA THREE

For each idea, write out the following:

Who's producing it.

When it will be completed.

The team involved.

The cost.

The objective (e-commerce, promotional, etc.).

What return on investment you expect – five new business meetings, three tweets, etc.

The completion date.

THINK CREATIVE GET CREATIVE BE CREATIVE

AFTERNOON TEA IN A BOX

We love to think creatively outside the box and look at what will excite a brand into working with us. Being an avid lover of afternoon tea, we came across the English Cream Tea Company – a beautiful creation of afternoon tea in a box, made fresh and delivered straight to your desk.

We had just had our new brochure created and rather than send it in the post, we wanted to think of a way that people would actually take the time to look at it. I had just been for a delicious afternoon tea at The Grove that weekend and what better way of creating a space for someone to take time out from their busy day than to send afternoon tea in a box and suggest that space can be made whilst sitting and reading the brochure.

Each box cost between £30 and £50, and we did a test run of 10 boxes to brands that we were very keen to engage with. Out of the first 10 boxes that we sent out, we had 9 people tweet the team box to all of their followers with pictures of them eating it and a thank you to the agency. We also booked in meetings immediately with four of the brands – one that we had been looking to work with as a high priority. When we went in to have the meeting, the brand representative mentioned that the tea box was great; however, the thing that grabbed his attention was our business card which he thought was so creative and well put together, and he knew that an agency with such considered branding and creative ways of approaching them must be worth a meeting.

We are now working with this company on a huge campaign for creative products and celebrity engagement not only here in the UK, but also engaging our LA office to launch the project in the USA. All in the name of afternoon tea!

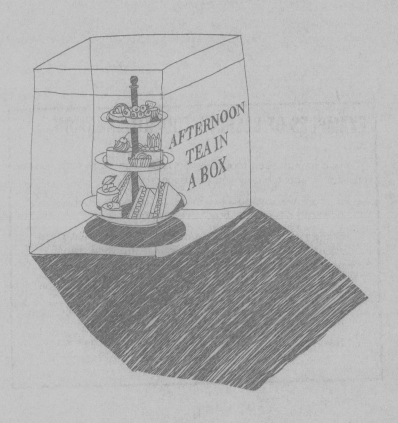

GREAT IDEA $\longrightarrow$ EXECUTION

WINNING

EXAMPLES OF BESPOKE TOOLKIT CREATION

—

You can look at each tool that you need to engage with your consumer and see how you can supersize it.

— If you have created a brochure, is there a way of turning this into a 3-minute brochure video?

— Could you create "common mistakes" videos that your clients will relate to as they are making those same mistakes videos?

— Perhaps your blog could be a video a day which can be sent straight to your customers' inbox.

— Brochure send out – how to engage your client.

— Invite creation and send out (think outside the box).

CREATING THE PRODUCT/SERVICES FOR YOUR BRAND

—

Okay, so now I get the toolkit creation but what about my product lines?

In discussion with brands about their product lines I regularly find myself coming up with the same questions:

01   Are you only providing a service but no product?

02   Are you aware that you can have a product line attached to the service that you offer?

03   Do you produce product first and then think about where you are going to sell it afterwards?

04   Is your product tailored to the target audience you have defined?

05   Has your team of product designers been briefed on your key messages/core values and target audience when putting together your range of products or services?

Product is key to the brand awareness and income stream of your business

A book is a product, CD box sets are products, live-streaming video via an e-commerce platform is a product, a 1:1 training session is a product, you can even be a product yourself. Look at David Beckham… he can sell himself and make money!

Have you ever found yourself dreaming of making money when you sleep? Wouldn't it be great to make money when you sleep and when you are awake? The quickest way of making that happen is to create different types of product line that generate income 24/7.

Nearly all businesses are able to offer a minimum of four different product lines, without which they could be missing out on additional income flowing through their business. In order to engage your ideal consumer and have them spend money on your product, you must think about why you have chosen that product/service and what the return on your investment will be when you put it out to market.

LINZIPEDIA: PRODUCT LINES

—

A product can be something you watch, touch, eat, smell, listen to, hold, converse with or a service provided – anything that you will earn money from.

#CREATE

CREATING PRODUCTS AND SERVICES WITH ONE BUSINESS MODEL

There are different types of product that will engage your end consumer. Have you ever heard people talking about B2B and B2C products?

B2B = selling from business to business.

B2C = selling from business to consumer (straight to the person and cutting out the business).

The old-school way of thinking was that you had to stay in one box rather than go from one to the other. But why not sell to both?

The new-school way allows you to cross-pollinate, selling through multiple product areas that will generate revenue through your business-to-business and/or business-to-consumer offerings.

The beauty of Internet shopping is that you are not reliant on other people selling your products. As long as you can design, produce and market your wares you can sell to whoever you want, whenever you want.

Treat the globe as your very own playground
Why don't we move into a space where you no longer think of product as a singular option? There are many types of product and there is no need to limit yourself to just one of them.

01 Physical product – something that you can see, touch and sell.

02 Service based – a service that you provide to your customers.

Have you ever considered creating a physical product if you are a service-based company or offering a service if you are a product-based business? Better still, how about creating products for prospective customers to engage with your bigger product offering?

CHART YOUR CURRENT PRODUCT/SERVICE

Write down which products and services you are offering/looking to offer within your business today:

PRODUCTS	SERVICES
01	01
02	02
03	03

The benefit of this game is to look at how your product/service offering can be adapted to create new areas of growth and enable you to extend your offering for tomorrow. The goal is to continue offering the existing product/service while starting to create new ones. Think of it like this, the people who are already buying your service will most likely benefit from any product that you can develop related to your service.

A simple multiplier effect shows that you can double the sales interaction from each potential existing customer by offering another product category. You can also open up to potential new customers by creating fresh product lines and later you will be able to upsell them into your existing service offering.

It is advisable that you keep the core service or product functioning and selling whilst beginning to expand into the other, so as to still generate income within the business unless you are just launching your brand and all your products/services are new. There are quick and simple ways in which to do this so that you grow both sides of your business. You must, however, always think about who your target audience is and why they are going to buy the products you are producing whilst always sticking to your – yes, you guessed it – key message and core values!

03 COMMON MISTAKES THAT PEOPLE MAKE WHEN TRYING TO EXTEND THEIR OFFERING

---

01 TARGETING THE WRONG AUDIENCE

This creates a ripple effect, whereby you don't have the sell-through/pick-up that you thought you would have as you have not joined the appropriate dots before going to market. The risk is that you waste time and money if you don't follow this process. It is great to have more than one product offering and to recognize that you have more than one target audience because this opens you up to a wider range of consumers. All you have to do is ensure that one is speaking to the other.

02 CONTINUING TO SPEAK TO THE EXISTING CUSTOMER WHEN CREATING A NEW PRODUCT RANGE

That is targeted at someone else. If you want to take your brand into a new target market it's important to do an evaluation process of who the new customer is and where they are positioned in the marketplace.

03 BUSINESSES GO TO MARKET WITH A NEW PRODUCT LINE TARGETED AT A NEW AGE OR DEMOGRAPHIC

Without communicating the concept to the rest of their sales and marketing team. In this case everyone, from the sales team to the PR department, continues talking to the younger consumer whilst selling the older product range offering and then the company is left scratching their heads and wondering why they are left with a warehouse full of product.

Before moving on to the product vision pyramid I would like to draw your attention to three essential ingredients when visualizing your product.

FUNCTION EQUALS POINT OF DIFFERENCE EQUALS DESIRE

—

FUNCTION

You may think that functionality is an obvious thing to mention; however, you must remember that your product function must be as obvious as what is written on the tin. If, as in my case, you are producing a clothing range then think – is this shoe something that can be worn, if that is not the function of the shoe then what is? If it is a plant pot then make sure that people are very aware that it is a plant pot to put plants in and not a shoe!

It may sound obvious, but you would not believe how many products go to market without the customer being clear what the product's intended use is. You know what happens then – a warehouse full of stock.

POINT OF DIFFERENCE

The second, and for me one of the most important points of all is "the point of difference". Paul Stead, well known in the industry for innovation/design gave me this great piece of advice to pass on to you. It means you should scour the market and be really really objective to ensure your product is different from the competition. The difference ideally should be more than aesthetic, it could be your business model your way of solving the problem. If in doubt ask the ultimate end user to tell you. And above all listen and learn from what they say.

DESIRE

You could say this is the sprinkle of icing sugar on the top. Desire sells product. When you have a product that works well (function) and has a unique point of difference, you will generate desire. If you have these three things you are on to a winner.

What is your product's point of difference? Why is it different from what is out in the marketplace at the moment? How does this create desire so your customer buys your product over something else?

THE BAROMETER OF BRAND FAME – CRONUT

—

BUILDING ON AN EXISTING HABIT TO PROVIDE A NEW NEED

—

Is it a donut? Is it a croissant? No, it's a cronut!

This new craze to hit the streets was a hybrid take on a croissant and a donut. Not my bag, but definitely building on a new need that is part of the fast food culture that is known and loved. When you see a cronut, it does make you wonder if it is a croissant or indeed a donut. This product definitely delivered on a strong point of difference that did not previously exist in the fast food sector. It created desire...

It literally took the USA by storm, featuring on most news channels, and found 200 people waiting in line for cronuts to open the doors to their first bakery. Whilst originally a single person could order six cronuts at a time, it has been reported that a limit of two cronuts per customer was being introduced for a period of time due to the craze that cronut mania created.

Victoria Beckham kicked off the hype on Twitter, posting a picture of herself eating one for breakfast, and the likes of Hugh Jackman were reportedly waiting in line for orders of cronuts.

All the publications and online blogs have been talking about it and tweeting it not only in the USA but around the world. The phenomenon has now travelled the globe and seen the Brits chase after the trend just like the Yanks. Five retail outlets have been opened, with more rumoured to come along and Selfridges selling them in their retail store.

The cronut delivered on a habit – or should I say an addiction – to fast food (namely the donut). Creating a point of difference, by blending it with a croissant, makes it stand out from the crowd and thus enables the cronut to tick all the boxes on the Barometer of Fame.

Change the rules so you control the rules. Play against your rules and not theirs.

Paul Stead
Innovator and world-class business leader

Who are you talking to with your product? Can you now see the relevance to this question?

If not, it's time to go back to the discover section.

With the end customer in mind, be prepared to focus on the key areas of your business that will generate the highest form of revenue and at the same time create huge awareness to drive traffic to your product. It is not always about selling highly priced products but ultimately it is about creating the awareness to drive traffic to the core product offering at the end of the process. Refer to your existing product/service chart to see where you are with your product before moving on to the next dot of creating new product lines.

It's nearly time to put your new product vision map together, but first let's take a look at the different types of product and service that are available to "productize" your brand. Here is a fact, most stand-out big brands today create more than one product line that speaks to different target customers.

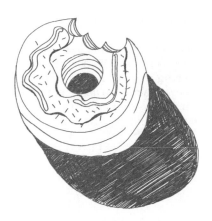

#CREATE

WORKING OUT YOUR PRODUCT OPTIONS

Brands today will recognize that in order to drive people to their core product line they need to create a platform through which they can engage with different groups of consumers. So, what are your options?

Product options come in all shapes and sizes – one size does not fit all. You will find on the Product Map on pages 120–21 a list of different product categories that new school brands today produce and engage with for their brand.

Before you turn over the page take a read of one of the product categories that you will find listed called Influencer product and see how important this can be when creating this for your brand.

THE IMPORTANCE OF THE INFLUENCER FOR BRANDS TODAY

Normally, the influencer area of a business will create awareness to drive traffic to the core collection, which then sells product in volumes. It requires people who do not have a celebrity status but are recognized within their industry or social circles, and change people's opinions when they are seen wearing a brand or using it.

Having an influencer audience for your influencer product keeps this product line exclusive, perhaps only featuring in high-end publications and seen being worn by A- and B-list celebrities as well as your influencer audience so as to maintain a luxury and high-end feel about it. This maintains the profile and aspirational elements of the brand.

HOW TO INFLUENCE

You may be wondering what effect this has on the rest of the brand. Using this influencer collection as a driver to elevate the awareness of the brand enables you to open your brand up to a wider audience and create awareness for an elite following or high-end audience that perhaps would not normally buy in to your range. You then bring in the mainstream collection that is accessible to all. The influencer collection has created the attention and awareness as a result of getting great coverage in high-end publications that the brand would not normally be seen in. The product is seen being worn by the right people and is placed in the best magazines, and retail stores are clamouring to buy your range. The knock-on effect is that mainstream stores, who know that they perhaps would not be able to sell the high-end product, still want a piece of the pie.

If you are reading this and thinking I don't need an influencer product then really have a think about whether or not your core product is going to create the attention that you need, not only through the press but also within the retail environment to create an awareness around the brand and more importantly a waiting list which will hopefully lead to ultimately selling out of your product. You may find that your core product has enough of an impact to make this happen, in which case you might look at producing a limited edition collection with a unique point of difference once this collection has reached its peak.

LINZIPEDIA: INFLUENCER

Someone that is known in the industry as a tastemaker/opinion former – not a follower but a leader in their industry or field. A person that is driven by style and not branding.

ADIDAS AND ITS INFLUENCER AUDIENCE

—

Adidas, for a number of years now, has been well known for creating a high-end/high-design sports range with Stella McCartney. I believe this was a way to create an influencer range within their main offering and it has been very well received.

This collaborative sports range, in the early stage of creation, would have been aware that it could only generate a small percentage of the main brand's income stream. It is a clever way of raising the profile and the awareness of the brand, and the high-end collection allows their brand to grace the pages of publications they would not necessarily be seen in and create a catwalk show that is held at the prestigious London Fashion Week to be attended by the influencer audience.

This in turn then drives sales to their mainstream customer. It also opens them up to high-end retailers such as Net-a-porter and Selfridges, which would not normally buy in to their brand in the designer area.

Most successful brands today recognize that having a premium product sends a trickle effect down to the mainstream consumer making their brand more desirable and more appealing to the masses. They can set a higher price point that appeals to the elite, cool set who are often seen wearing it not often for the label but usually for the design/kudos.

HIGHER-END RETAIL STORES PROVIDE THE PERFECT RETAIL ENVIRONMENT TO SELL THE INFLUENCER COLLECTION FROM.

your
brand
here

WHAT PRODUCT AM I?

Influencer product

These create a spike of awareness around your brand and can be limited edition or a permanent range collaborating with someone to raise their profile (e.g., a high-end designer, famous product designer, well-known professional or an opinion former to design, create or endorse the product). Coca cola did this well recently, with Karl Lagerfeld as the designer of their can for a limited range that sold through the likes of Harvey Nichols.

Mainstream product

Sells mass volume by targeting a more accessible audience, appealing to a much wider consumer who looks to invest in the brand as a whole, but not necessarily buy in to the higher-end designer pieces from an influencer product range. They will, though, buy in to hype that has been driven by the influencer collection which in turn filters down to the mainstream product.

Innovation product

A product that has been created with a unique point of difference that will be a game changer in changing the way we think, act and behave. The best example for this is the one that everyone knows, Apple.

Technical product

A product line created in the realms of sport, technology and any other area that has a technical use for delivery – for example, Nike + iPod sensor in their shoe that will track your running. A lot of brands are moving into a technical product space as they see it as the way of the future. Using the same principles as above, except this time using influential sports people to sell the technical collection and allow the customer to buy in to the dream. Again Nike does this so well; think back if you can to the Air Jordan shoe and how many millions that trainer sold off the back of Michael Jordan's name and amazing basketball skills.

Information product

Products created to provide information. They come in the shape of books, e-books, DVDs, education systems, online platforms and members' areas, for example. This is a great way of incorporating an information product within your core offering that should guarantee you a wider range of sales while you sleep.

Education product

These can come in the form of information products and are used on the same platforms as above. They can also be run through seminars, events and coaching/education programmes that lead to larger education courses.

Expert product

Creating yourself as an expert in your field can be a product in its own right; you may feel like you are not an expert and someone out there is more knowledgeable in the subject than you are. This could well be true, but as long as your profile, social media and product lines are more in the public eye, he doesn't stand a chance. Whatever you feel your specialist subject is, ensure that you have enough knowledge in this area to write and talk about it with a real voice of authority.

Affiliate product

This is a referral product that enables you to make money in the form of commissions, percentages or referral fees. You refer people to product lines that already exist and create an income stream from your site to theirs. The best way of doing this is by actually creating an affiliate website of your own.

Service-based product

This first-hand product is commonly termed "one on one". This can be working as a personal trainer (PT), therapist (physical or other), life coach, accountant or tutor. You can earn from this as much as you can physically fit into a day. Your price is dependent on your offering and I know people that charge £3000 per hour and others that charge £30. The £30 an hour person will have very little time to grow his business, needing to work all the hours he can find, whereas the £3000 an hour person only needs to work a few hours and spend the rest of his time building a famous brand.

White-label product

Products or services that are created by someone else and re-branded by another company to look like their own. A brand can expand their own product offering by investing in product directly from a factory/manufacturer/producer and putting their own branding on it (i.e. "white labelling") whilst adding a mark-up of no less than 15% (the industry standard), leaving you with a ready-made product line without having to create and produce the line.

GAME 04
CREATE YOUR
PRODUCT VISION PYRAMID

I suggest that now is a good time to plot out your product vision pyramid detailing which products and services you are able to offer within your business today.

Take a look back at the products and services chart you wrote down in DOT Game 03. Review where you could add in any extra products and services to be able to create more opportunity to reach out to your end consumer.

You should now be looking to create a pyramid where you can provide your end consumer with some education product, affiliate product, white label product, influencer product, mainstream and affiliate products. If you find another product area relevant for your business then please include it in your pyramid – this has been given as a guide to get you started.

HAVE A LOOK AT THE #BRANDFAMOUS PRODUCT PYRAMID TO GET AN IDEA OF WHAT YOUR PRODUCT PYRAMID COULD LOOK LIKE, THEN MAP YOURS OUT INTO THE PYRAMID CHART ON THE NEXT PAGE...

HOW A PRODUCT PYRAMID COULD LOOK

Indicator

FREE

DVD box set
Online members
Information product

LOW PRICE

Affiliate product
Affiliate marketing

LOW–MEDIUM PRICE

Education programme
Course
Workshop
Online education
Services

MEDIUM–HIGH PRICE

Influence product
LB presents
Ltd. edition
Capsule collection
Celebrity product

HIGH PRICE

Online retail
E-comm/M-comm white label product

CREATE YOUR OWN HERE

FREE

LOW PRICE

LOW–MEDIUM PRICE

MEDIUM–HIGH PRICE

HIGH PRICE

ONE

FINAL WORD

IN THE WORLD WE ARE LIVING IN RIGHT NOW, THE MAINSTREAM CUSTOMERS ARE INFLUENCED BY CELEBRITY, DESIGNER OR SPORTING TALENT AND IN THE CASE OF A FAMOUS SPORTS PERSON'S RANGE WANT TO EMULATE THEIR FAVOURITE FOOTBALL, TENNIS OR GOLF STAR AND BE MADE TO FEEL LIKE THEY ARE PART OF THE TRIBE. BUYING IN TO THEIR FAVOURITE CELEB LINE THROUGH THE BRAND MAKES THEM FEEL LIKE THEY ARE ONE STEP CLOSER TO THEIR FAVOURITE SPORTING LEGEND. KA-CHING!

YOU NOW HAVE AN IDEA OF WHAT PRODUCT VISION YOU HAVE AT THE MOMENT AND WHAT TYPE OF PRODUCT YOU ARE LOOKING TO CREATE; HOWEVER, I AM SURE THAT YOU ARE STILL WONDERING HOW AND WHERE YOU CAN GO ABOUT GETTING THIS DONE.

#CREATE

DEFINING WHERE BEST TO PRODUCE YOUR PRODUCT

"Sewing" the seed for production
You may now be interested in producing a product range but have no manufacturing knowledge. When I owned my footwear brand we sold 150,000 pairs of shoes in the first season, selling through 7 different distribution channels on a global scale. We did not know that this would happen when we launched the product at our first trade show. We took an order with a German distributor for 40,000 pairs of shoes. This meant we were able to produce the shoes in Korea, which came with a lower price point but a higher minimum order quantity per style and colour. Also, the shipping took two months to arrive and we air-freighted in product to satisfy the demand through retail so as not to dampen the hype that had been created through the press and to deliver on the waiting list that had built up at retail.

Fast-forward to today and the Internet has made the world a much smaller place. There are great places to search for manufacturing, so that you can easily access product without having the expense of flight, travel and communication costs.

PAUSE FOR THOUGHT

A small peek into the future...
It will be interesting to see how the world changes over the next 10 years. There is a 3D scanner in existence that can produce a 3D product by scanning a drawing into the machine. I imagine that this will become so mainstream a few years from now that you will be able to produce your own product from the comfort of your living room.

WHERE TO PRODUCE THE PRODUCT

ARE YOU LOOKING FOR HIGH VOLUME LOW COST PRODUCT

ARE YOU LOOKING FOR LOW VOLUME AND MEDIUM COST

DO YOU NEED QUICK TURNAROUND PRODUCTION?

ARE YOU ABLE TO HAVE TWO TO THREE MONTHS LEAD TIME FOR SHIPPING

WILL YOU PAY EXTRA TO HAVE PRODUCT AIR-FREIGHTED IN?

ARE SMALL MINIMUMS MORE APPEALING TO YOU?

If you have answered yes to high volume and low cost and are happy to either wait for shipping or pay a bit extra for sending product in by air then look at production in the Middle East.

If you are sitting on the more cautious side of production, want to road test the product without having to order much stock and are keen to have shorter production lead times so you can get orders in quickly if you start to takeon bigger orders then producing closer to home will suit you better.

GLOBAL PRODUCTION JUST GOT SMALLER: PRODUCING IN THE MIDDLE EAST MADE EASIER

––––

Alibaba is an online platform that has become popular to source production in China and the Middle East. You must remember that although price points can be low for samples, minimum order quantities can be high per style and per colour, with shipping and duty costly if delivering to Europe and the UK. When this is the case, many businesses tend to bring product in via boat to keep the cost down. However, this is a slow process and can take up to two months, which affects the time the retailer has to sell the product!

The beauty of producing in China is the low cost/high volume yet, unless you have a ready-made order to put alongside it, this way can be costly and timely. If, like us, you are sitting with an order book of 150,000 pairs of shoes and a distribution channel ready to go, or your testing process through the Internet was successful, it is worth looking at the Middle East or Asia since the production costs and quality can far outweigh what European manufacturing has to offer.

Localize your production for ease

The UK and Europe have a strong manufacturing industry and, although the price points tend to be higher, this is balanced out with the lower cost of shipping and the reduced time delay on product production. It also involves much less expense for travelling when you are a smaller business. The minimums tend to be lower, so a small to medium-sized business can look to create a sample collection and sell a much lower volume product to limited retail outlets and create an e-commerce platform to maximize the higher percentage of profit that can be created from going direct from factory to your own store. The beauty of today is that you don't need the high rents of the high street to create an income stream with low overheads.

TIP

Go on LinkedIn and there are loads of networks now that show lists of great factories in the UK and Europe where you can get product produced.

How do I know whether to produce in a far-reached factory such as in the Middle East or produce near to home?
One thing to bear in mind, whether you are producing in the Middle East or Europe you will still have setup costs to consider and with innovation/technology products requiring special tooling, this could make your start-up costs exceptionally high as opposed to information product which, although time consuming to create, is low cost in terms of production and reasonably fast to manufacture. With most products, ask about a way of amortizing your setup costs into the unit price per product in production – the higher the volume you produce, the lower the setup unit cost going onto each item.

LB SUGGESTS

You might want to think about the fact that you would be expected to place a minimum order of around 300 per style in the Middle East and around 100 per style in Europe – a big difference for a smaller company with fewer ways to distribute.

#CREATE

SAMPLING YOUR PRODUCT

Before you move on to Step 03: Connect, you need to have a sample of the product that you want to sell in order to review what your options are for sales and to be able to get some orders placed.

When it comes to looking at sampling, I draw on my experience of working in the world of fashion. I have seen the sheer number of designs, patterns and fabric offerings that are needed in order to produce samples. A fashion brand has to deliver a whole new collection of different styles into store four times a year due to the demand of retail and the consumer wanting fresh product delivered often. In the fashion world there is constant research taking place, watching and delivering on latest trends, recognizing new innovations in fabric and design to keep the designer/brand at the head of their game. High-street stores (the brands) have to be quick to get the new trends in store; they look to the catwalks and trend agencies and recreate the latest ideas themselves at a much lower price and sometimes get the product out before the designers themselves.

Can you imagine if fast-moving consumer brands had to design and deliver on four new product lines a year with approximately 20 new styles minimum in the range? Imagine also needing to get them into store quickly enough so that a high-street store does not show the trend first. Something tells me they would all struggle to stay in business.

Design first, sample second

Firstly, if you have not done so already, think about who is going to design/illustrate your product. If you are not part of a big team then look to use a freelance designer. Ask them to show you a portfolio of work they have designed in the past; make sure that they have some design work that is relevant for your product needs.

It really is trial and error, as there are endless designers, illustrators and product developers out there. So, look for someone who is not only best suited to design your product but also able to ensure that the factory knows what the dimensions of the product and the material requirements are so that the sampling is made easier and endless attempts do not have to be made.

The joys of sampling

Sampling is a laboured job in any product category and each comes with its own problems. Food and drink have meticulous health and safety issues, which mean long and laborious documentation at each different stage of production in the factory.

Quality control is as important as the product design itself. In this early sampling stage, assessing and road testing the product is essential so that when going into production, and potentially spending large amounts of money on moulds and machinery, you are able to make sure that the product is not going to fail on quality. Quality control early on will enable you to sidestep the horror that brands see where whole shipments of product are returned by the retailer due to faulty batches of orders received.

Finally, understand the numbers behind your product so that you know from research and not guesswork what size, colour or shape you should be ordering. When we produced our shoes we were very aware of the packs of shoe sizes to sell in to retail stores so they did not get stuck with sizes.

Research what the market is looking for today. It is forever changing, with people's wants, needs and size/shape affecting what the retailer is able to sell.

MR MOO
AND FRIENDS

I had a two-year stint at sampling, producing and testing my own baby food range called Mr Moo and Friends on the famous market stalls of Stroud, Gloucestershire. I knew nothing about food production – least of all for kids, which is a high-risk area. I had to go on numerous health and hygiene courses to even get started with the sampling process and produce the range. During the sampling stage we tested the different product lines multiple times, with my son's friends delivering the samples to their houses with questionnaires to receive feedback from their young taste buds. We wanted to see which ones were eaten and which were thrown on the floor!

Once we had the range of 12 we then turned my kitchen at home into a sterile environment to the standard of any working factory, which saw me dressed up like a dinner lady – white hat, coat and shoes. We then spent a year testing the product on the market and getting feedback on what worked and what didn't.

I found that I had reached the point where I wanted to take it to the supermarkets and, despite it having great traction with sales, I wanted to educate myself more in delivering a famous brand so when I was ready, it too would be ready. Not a brand to turn famous yet, but one that is still a work in progress…

GAME 06
ASSESS AND ROAD TEST YOUR PRODUCT

—

Five things to consider when sampling your product

01 IF YOU ARE PRODUCING A PRODUCT FROM SCRATCH

This will need to be created either at a local or a far-flung factory where, in either case, your sample costs need to be paid upfront.

02 DEPENDING ON THE PRODUCT, YOU WILL NORMALLY BE ASKED TO ALSO PUT DOWN TOOLING OR MOULD COSTS IF IT IS BESPOKE TO YOU

This can be extremely costly, so make sure you are able to show them from an existing picture or a drawing with measurements what you want so that they are able to get the sample right first time.

03 SAMPLE, SAMPLE, SAMPLE until you get it right.

Don't settle on the first one – I can only imagine how many times Dyson sampled their product before getting it right.

04 TEST THE QUALITY OF THE PRODUCT

... more than once so that you are 100% sure that when you go into production and out to retail, you are not going to be left with a load of returns. This will affect both your relationship with the retailer and your profit – you won't make any money if everything is sent back.

05 DON'T GIVE UP

If at first you don't succeed, try, try again. Many a collection has been thrown in the bin when the samples have arrived only to start again and turn out to become a famous brand. Rome wasn't built in a day.

I HOPE THAT THIS CREATE SECTION HAS SHOWN THAT THERE IS HUGE OPPORTUNITY TO CREATE A BROADER DEPTH OF PRODUCT IN YOUR BRAND. YOU MAY HAVE BEEN TRADING FOR A NUMBER OF YEARS NOW; IMAGINE EXPLORING FURTHER WHAT THESE PRODUCT OPPORTUNITIES COULD LOOK LIKE FOR YOU, AND THEN CONSIDER THE BENEFITS WHEN CONNECTING MULTIPLE PRODUCT LINES TO RETAIL. YOU MAY ALSO HAVE NOTICED FROM DISSECTING YOUR BRAND UP TO THIS POINT THAT YOU HAVE EXPANDED YOUR CLIENT BASE BUT STILL ONLY OFFER ONE TYPE OF PRODUCT OR SERVICE.

AS YOU LEAVE THE CREATE PHASE, YOU WILL HOPEFULLY NOW FIND YOURSELF IN A PLACE OF HAVING GREAT IDEAS AROUND DIFFERENT TYPES OF PRODUCT YOU CAN SAMPLE. THE FOLLOWING CHAPTER WILL ENABLE YOU TO FIGURE OUT WHERE AND HOW YOU ARE GOING TO GENERATE ORDERS AND FUNDS SO THAT YOU CAN THEN PLACE A SIZEABLE ORDER WITH THE FACTORY. IT WILL GIVE YOU A CLEARER UNDERSTANDING OF WHAT MINIMUMS YOU WILL REQUIRE, HOW YOU ARE GOING TO RETAIL, WHO IS GOING TO BUY THE PRODUCT, HOW TO PRICE YOUR PRODUCT FOR THE MARKETPLACE AND HOW MUCH STOCK YOU NEED TO PLACE TO SATISFY THE DEMAND YOU HAVE CREATED.

QUICK PEEK CHEAT SHEET

—

WHAT WE HAVE CREATED

01 WORKING OUT WHERE YOU ARE TODAY WITH YOUR PRODUCT/SERVICE
CREATE YOUR ESSENTIAL TOOLKIT

—

02 GETTING THE MOST FROM YOUR TOOLKIT
CREATE YOUR OWN BESPOKE MODEL

—

03 CREATING PRODUCTS AND SERVICES WITH ONE BUSINESS MODEL
CHART YOUR CURRENT PRODUCT/SERVICE

—

04 WORKING OUT YOUR PRODUCT OPTIONS
CREATE YOUR PRODUCT VISION PYRAMID

—

05 DEFINING WHERE BEST TO PRODUCE YOUR PRODUCT
WHERE TO PRODUCE YOUR PRODUCT

—

06 SAMPLING YOUR PRODUCT
ASSESS AND ROAD TEST YOUR PRODUCT

—

Enter your information at the school of brand fame to gain more insight and also a game summary.
www.brandfamous.com/schoolofbrandfame

CHAPTER 06:
STEP THREE #CONNECT

—

CONNECTING YOUR PRODUCT
TO YOUR AUDIENCE

—

Enter into the … CONNECT PHASE

If you have followed the programme up to here you have already done a great deal more than many businesses out in the marketplace today, so pause for a moment to congratulate yourself on a job well done. You are very much on the way to building your famous brand.

I would like to invite you to consider how you are going to connect your product to a sales channel. This connect phase is a chapter that will allow you to open your mind to doing just that. How are you going to sell your product once it has been produced and what are the options available to you? It looks at selling business to business and also business to consumer, whilst looking at both an online e-commerce site and a retail channel and what the pros and cons are for each. This chapter will provide you with a chance to look at how to test your product without committing to big stock quantities that could sit in your warehouse or back bedroom gathering dust as you try to figure out who will buy your product.

Have you ever thought it would be great to be given practical information that could be put into action straight away through your existing/new sales channel. I think you will find that this section of the book gives you just that.

THE BODY TRANSFORMATION COACH

—

At one point I worked with a client who had a very successful body transformation business – his clients were achieving huge weight-loss transformations in four-week periods, following a review of their diets and supplements and by devising an effective weight-lifting programme.

Owing to his success rate with clients, he had a ready-made clientele and a waiting list for his services. However, after some analysis, he realized that each client was spending a minimum of £100 per month on supplements which he was referring them to buy elsewhere, on top of their training programmes. He had a small team consisting of himself and two other trainers who were all using these supplements on their clients. Between them they were working 60 clients at a time. After working out the maths, we realized that he should create and offer his own small supplement range. We created a range of the highest quality food-based organic grade and found a local manufacturer to produce it.

Within one month of launch he was making £5000 per month from the supplement sales alone with his existing client base, without taking into account the personal training fees that he was charging as his core product. He then created an e-book, an e-commerce site, became an expert in a key men's publication for fitness and online blogs. Once recognized for his work his supplement sales tripled in size overnight (refer to product map in create section…tick, tick, tick).

PLAY THE CONNECT DOT-TO-DOT GAME

—

DOT 01

FINDING A BUYER AND YOUR NICHE

—

GAME 01A
DEFINE WHO YOUR PRODUCT IS SELLING TO (B2B AND B2C)

GAME 01B
DEFINE THE PRODUCT TO CREATE

**GETTING READY
TO PRODUCE YOUR
PRODUCT**
—

GAME 04
**DECIDE WHERE AND
HOW TO PRODUCE YOUR
PRODUCT LINES**

**BUILDING CONFIDENCE
WHEN PRICING**
—

GAME 03
**GET RETAILER INSIGHT INTO
YOUR COSTING MODEL**

**KNOW YOUR PLACE IN
THE RETAIL SPACE: B2B
MADE FUN**
—

GAME 02A
SET YOUR RETAIL OBJECTIVES

GAME 02B
**CONNECT YOUR PRODUCT
TO RETAIL**

#CONNECT
___

FINDING A BUYER AND YOUR NICHE
___

There are three things to be aware of when thinking about the next steps of creating your products and connecting them to your end consumer.

01 Find a buyer to sell to
Be wary of creating your product first and seeking someone to buy it second. The best way to think about creating product is to look at who you are already targeting – it's easier to fill demand than it is to create it.

02 Find your niche and stick with it
When thinking about the product you want to create, think about the niche audience you are selling to. The body transformation coach above targeted people who wanted to get a result in four weeks with a lasting impact – so he went for body builders who wanted to lose a percentage of fat quickly, post-pregnancy women, as well as women and men who would have extreme results that could be showcased as a before-and-after case study. The supplements were a definitive way of promoting the body transformations as a necessary "tool" for success.

Creating your niche, going deeper into it and really taking ownership of your space in that niche is a sure fire way of being a big fish in a small pond. It is always better to be a big fish in a small pond than a small fish swimming around getting lost in a big one!

03 Short lead time on orders – producing locally
If you are not getting retail stores to buy your product and you don't want to place an order of product before you have tested the product out online, find a factory that can produce and ship the product with a four-week lead time. This way you can be promoting your sample collection for sale online and placing an order direct with the factory once you have hit the minimum that allows you to break even so you are not losing any money.

GAME 01A
DEFINE WHO YOUR PRODUCT IS SELLING TO (B2B AND B2C)

—

The first key to get things moving is to look back at your product vision map from the create section and take a look at who you are targeting with your products.

01 WRITE DOWN ON YOUR PRODUCT VISION MAP NEXT TO EACH PRODUCT CATEGORY WHETHER THE PRODUCTS ARE B2B OR B2C.

02 HOW DO YOU INTEND TO SELL YOUR PRODUCTS?

03 ARE YOU LOOKING TO SELL DIRECTLY INTO YOUR CLIENT BASE OR THROUGH YOUR E-COMMERCE SITE OR WILL YOU GO DIRECT TO RETAIL?

You may be wondering how to get started? You have hopefully got your product to a point where it is ready to go; you have samples ready to sell, or an idea of what they are, designed and drawn up in a CAD (computer aided design) drawing that at the least represents a high enough quality for people to buy or gauge a reaction from. It's now time to look at what options you have for sale.

There are many options of where and how to sell, and I would say that you should explore what works for you and your audience (mapped out in DOT Game 01a). The old-school way was for B2B businesses to sell only to businesses and never consider selling to the consumer. Please know that in today's evolution of a brand there are no rules. You are now free to rewrite the rulebook and sell to both – this is the way forward for modern brands. If you are a B2C business look hard for the B2B opportunities, it is not as difficult as you might think. One of the easiest ways is through the education and information product – teach what you know best and find the niche in that.

WHETHER SELLING TO A BUSINESS, THROUGH A RETAILER OR DIRECT TO THE END CUSTOMER YOU NEED TO BE AWARE OF WHAT YOUR OPTIONS ARE.

GAME 01B
DEFINE THE PRODUCT TO CREATE

—

Based on your product vision map, write out which product you have decided to create first and what target audience each product would be speaking to.

— How many new lines/services do you want to produce?

— Which products will make a difference in your market-place?

— Is there an influencer product and a mainstream one that you want to produce?

— Is this talking to your existing customer or a new one?

PRODUCT

TARGET AUDIENCE

#CONNECT

KNOW YOUR PLACE IN THE RETAIL SPACE: B2B MADE FUN

If you are a business that has products to sell direct to other businesses then those products could be categorized, as I mentioned in the create section, for example, as an education product, a white label product or some affiliate product to get you started.

Online education is a low-cost way of creating product and infiltrating your audience. It is relatively easy to put together an e-book or an online video, even with an iPhone from the comfort of your own living room. These are great tools to offer information to your existing database of clients. You can also look to provide potential clients with this as a free gift to build a following to sell your bigger offering to.

You may have a product you want others to sell for you; this can be made lucrative for them by offering an affiliate deal. This can be in the form of a package deal, such as "buy 10 and pay for 7" so that the affiliate can sell the product on with a mark-up, or you can set up an affiliate programme from your website so that they can make a percentage for every sale made. Make sure you make it worth their while to sell your product.

The above can make for lucrative business, especially if you have an existing strong database of clients for pre-orders. It also enables you to use them as one of your channels for (a) testing your product and (b) getting money upfront to pay for the product before committing to big orders.

Test before you invest

Testing the product out in the market is a great way of assessing what the demand is like and if the retail price is accurate. Before producing your product, advertise it to your existing database and have them place their orders. Then, using the profit to order extra stock, place your order with the factory so you never run at a loss. This will also generate a waiting list; a great thing to leak to journalists, so they believe there is a high demand and desirability for your brand.

Opening the doors to retail

Retail stores have buyers, these are the people who will ultimately invest in your product in their store and normally make a forward order with a three- to six-month lead time. These buyers are inundated with hundreds of products on a monthly basis and it can sometimes be hard to get your product seen. I find that without direct contact with the buyer you have to use different ways to engage them and grab their attention.

You will find it harder to convince retailers to buy in to your product lines if your toolkit (from the create section) does not give them clear information about what you are selling to them. In order to engage a retailer to get your product seen, you must think about:

— Still life images (creative look book).

— Information on the product line.

— Biography of the creator.

— His/her credibility in the marketplace.

LINZIPEDIA: CREATIVE LOOK BOOK

—

Something that will catch the attention of a buyer. You could use creative packaging – send it on an iPad, build a model in 3D; anything that will grab the attention of the buyer.

Consider where and how you see your product positioned in the marketplace so as to easily convince any retail buyer to take a look at your brand. It is essential to know the unit cost of the product and to have made a price comparison of other brands that sit in the buyer's store. Even if you purposefully desire a higher price point you need to know that the retailer can accommodate that.

The more engaging your creative look book the better, as this showcases your product range and should be able to grab the attention of the buyer. Bear in mind that they literally get hundreds of products sent through on a monthly basis, so please make yours stand out from the crowd. It is essential to stay on brand with the look and feel of your product. Get this right and you will be able to use it again for the communicate section which we are coming to next.

On the off chance that you remain unsuccessful in this regard and are keen to sell into retail, then you can always employ an agent who has the contacts and can almost guarantee access to the big retail stores. Sounds great you say, the downside, however is that the agent will charge you between 15% and 20% for the privilege, rendering your profit margin even smaller.

The benefits of having a retailer are that you will get a guaranteed order upfront, enabling you to place your product order with the factory. Having longer lead times means that you can have the product produced in the Middle East, providing you can meet the order minimums, which means that your unit price would come down considerably and you would have time to ship it, which is cheaper than air freight.

A big slice of the pie

Expect the retailer to take a huge slice of the profit. For the retailer to sell the product they will want a minimum of three times the cost price mark. Say you can produce something at £3.00 and want to sell it at £19.99. With a RRP (recommended retail price) of £19.99, you would need to sell the product to the retailer for £6.50, making you a profit of £3.50 and the retailer a profit of £13.99. This equation has not taken into account the VAT/tax situation, which differs from country to country.

Research on different types of retailer is imperative – even knowing the basics of how many stores they own will enable you to assess if they are the right store for your product and when they do order, what quantity you can expect them to place. If you are targeting stores that are only going to place small orders due to their minimal distribution channels (they may only have one or two shops, for instance), you should be aware that you will need to engage more retail stores to buy your product so that you can cover all your manufacturing minimums without any cost to yourself.

My advice would first be to set your retail objectives: know what it is you want to achieve in your retail vision and then formulate your plan of attack. Then, evaluate the process to successfully implement the procedure. Without setting and planning your retail objectives you risk not getting the project off the ground.

SET YOUR RETAIL OBJECTIVES

Here are four key questions to ask yourself when setting your retail objectives:

01 WHAT WOULD YOU LIKE TO ACHIEVE WITH YOUR VENTURE INTO RETAIL?

02 DO YOU WANT TO GROW THE BRAND INTO DIFFERENT AREAS TO INFILTRATE NEW RETAIL SPACES?

03 WOULD YOU LIKE TO FOCUS ON JUST THE TOP 10 RETAIL STORES IN YOUR FIELD TO SET THE PRECEDENT FOR YOUR BRAND AND ENGAGE AN INFLUENCER AUDIENCE?

04 ARE YOU LOOKING AT MASS DISTRIBUTION THROUGH ONE RETAIL STORE WHICH HAS MULTIPLE RETAIL OUTLETS NATIONWIDE, OR A NUMBER OF SMALL RETAIL STORES OR BOTH?

LB SUGGESTS

If you decide to sell through retail and on your own e-commerce site, make sure you all sell to the end consumer at the same price. Provide a RRP that everyone sticks to.

Now you have a wider understanding of where and why you would like to distribute your product, let's take a look at owning your own retail store in the clouds...

Cloud nine: Owning your own retail. E-commerce made easy

The beauty of selling through your own e-commerce store is that you are now in charge of your own distribution destiny. It does, however, come with its own pros and cons: you have to consider how you are going to ship your product once you have taken an order. This can be done via your own means, inside your office or warehouse or by employing the services of a pick-and-pack company who will do it for you for a very small piece of the pie. You will find many based in your area on Google. Alternatively, your factory might be able to provide you with that service at an extra cost per unit, which would always be my preferred choice.

Selling direct from e-commerce means no guaranteed upfront order to enable you to place your initial order with the factory, unless of course you tested the product out in the marketplace first. However, your profit margin will increase in contrast with retail. With costs of £3.00, selling on your e-commerce platform at £19.99 means the difference between the two numbers goes into your pocket. A huge difference, but more risk.

There is now a great way of using your online e-commerce site as a way to test the marketplace with your product.

— If you are white labelling someone else's product, this is an easy way to utilize the Internet without having any lead times for production.

— Use pay per click advertising with Google and on targeted sites, including eBay and any social media pages, to speak to your niche audience to drive traffic to your product. Once someone clicks on the advert they are sent to your own e-commerce site to place the order where the payment is automatically taken from a card. This is also a great way to data capture people's contact details!

Once a week the orders are then sent over to the manufacturer of the product and sent direct to the customer with you paying the manufacturer as little as 40% to 60% of the retail price.

If you are testing your own product pre-production, it is advisable to list on the site that delivery will take up to four weeks (or however long it takes to produce locally, with short lead times on production and shipping).

GAME 02B
CONNECT YOUR PRODUCT
TO RETAIL
—

01 WRITE OUT THREE GOALS THAT WILL ENABLE YOU TO SET UP A DISTRIBUTION CHANNEL THROUGH B2B AND/OR B2C.

02 FOR EACH GOAL, WRITE OUT FIVE TO TEN STEPS IN WHICH YOU ARE GOING TO MAKE THIS GOAL HAPPEN.

#CONNECT

___

BUILDING CONFIDENCE WHEN PRICING

___

Finally, before you sell your product via any of the above three channels or before testing your samples in the marketplace, be prepared to do a competitor analysis to see the price that similar products are being sold for. I would suggest looking at a minimum of three different retail stores or e-commerce sites for comparison. This enables you to go to a retailer with a RRP and ensures you meet the retailer's pricing expectations without jeopardizing your own profit margin. Retailers will be unlikely to cut their own margins to accommodate you. They will want to know if you have any minimum order restrictions, what the shipping costs to them will be (if included), what the delivery dates and payment terms are. If it's one of the more desirable or high-demand stores, they will have their own criteria that you will have to meet. It is fine not to have all the answers to the questions as long as you go into the meeting fully prepared and stand in a place of authority with all the facts and figures you need to back yourself up. This will then show that you have done your research and gathered sufficient information to encourage the retailer to write and place an order. The main goal when selling to retail is to walk away with a confirmed order, so spend some time working out what it takes to make that happen.

Delivering on time
One thing to bear in mind when selling to any of the above is delivering on time. Your brand does not want to suffer from bad online rating or retailers returning or refusing product for not hitting the delivery date. This will not only ruin the reputation of your brand but also send your cash flow into a frenzy as you will be left with a lot of unwanted stock that would need to be sold off at a reduced price – this is not ideal for a new product launch to market.

GAME 03
GET RETAILER INSIGHT
INTO YOUR COSTING MODEL

—

Refer back to your product vision plan and, once you have done that, carry out a quick search on the Internet to see what other products, similar to yours, are in the marketplace. Use the chart below to work out the cost price, profit margin and retail price of your product.

COST PRICE

WHOLESALE

PROFIT

RETAIL PRICE

A little calculation needed

Doing this exercise will enable you to have a clearer picture of what your profit margin could look like and, if it is a high-volume product with a high profit margin, you are on to a winner!

Look at the cost price to buy your samples from the factory, the volume you expect to sell and where you think you will sell it. Your own online store will provide a bigger profit margin; however, you need to have a strong marketing campaign to drive consumers to your site. Once you have worked this out, you will then know what kind of profit you can make and how much money you have to spend on toolkit creation, marketing and PR to drive sales to your retail outlet.

One final thing – know what you are selling, how you are selling it and the pricing mechanism that sits around it. When you do get that meeting with the retailer or business you want to sell into, be prepared. You only get one chance at selling product to them and trust me, your product is only important to you at this stage and not them. What will you do to turn the tables?

#CONNECT

GETTING READY TO PRODUCE YOUR PRODUCT

You have now come to the end of the connect section. In order for you to move on to the next chapter, communicate, you should now have an understanding of what types of product there are, which product lines you are going to produce, if you are going to create new target groups and how you are going to sell your product to your end consumer.

Have clear steps forward
You will soon realize that taking those vital steps forward – no matter how big or small – is better than taking no steps once you have your targets set. You can aim high, reach for the stars, set huge expectations and then take the big picture and break it down so you can take baby steps on a daily, weekly and monthly basis that will eventually get you to your destination.

Don't miss those little successes...
Within your plan you can write out what the small wins and the big wins might look like for you so you can recognize them and celebrate the fact that you have reached your destination, even if it is only for a moment before setting off on your journey again. Small steps lead to success and keep you motivated to keep on and aim higher – once you become aware of your wins, as opposed to focusing always on the next challenge ahead, you will start to feel a sense of achievement and the motivation to keep going and move faster will be present.

Your own feeling of failure will always challenge your mindset, so keep checking in with the successes you achieve on a regular basis. This will keep you motivated to move forward. There is nothing that can hold you back other than your own fear of failure. So, as you tick off each step and notice you are already winning, your successes will soon override your failures and eliminate your once-irrational fears. If the game is being played all out, you cannot lose. The destination has been set and you are going for it. Remember, once you are happy with the objectives that you have set for your business, it's a game for you to win.

If you are still feeling unsure and are nervous about going into production, or you would like to check in and make sure that you are clear on all the points that have been provided in the connect section, then play this last game where you will answer a number of questions to help you decide on where and how to produce your product lines.

DECIDE WHERE AND HOW
TO PRODUCE YOUR PRODUCT LINES

—

Ask yourself whether you are ready to produce
your product:

IS THERE A DEMAND FOR YOUR PRODUCT? HAVE YOU AN END CUSTOMER ALREADY LINED UP TO BUY YOUR PRODUCT?

ARE YOU CLEAR ON THE TYPE OF VOLUME YOU EXPECT THEM TO BUY SO YOU CAN PLACE YOUR ORDER — WILL IT BE ONE BIG ORDER OR LOTS OF SMALL ONES?

HAVE YOU TESTED YOUR PRODUCT IN THE MARKET TO SEE IF THERE IS A DEMAND OR DO YOU HAVE A READY-MADE AUDIENCE WILLING TO BUY INTO THE LINES?

HAVE YOU DONE A PRICE ANALYSIS OF YOUR PRODUCT IN THE MARKETPLACE? DO YOU KNOW WITH CONFIDENCE WHAT YOUR PRODUCT WILL SELL FOR?

ARE YOU NOW CLEAR ON THE EXPECTED VOLUME THAT YOU WILL LOOK TO SELL PER STYLE AND COLOUR SO YOU CAN, WITH CONFIDENCE, PLACE YOUR ORDER WITH THE FACTORY?

ARE YOU NOW CLEAR ON WHICH FACTORY IS GOING TO BE THE RIGHT ONE FOR YOU? LOCAL OR MIDDLE EAST?

YOU WILL WANT TO PRESENT TWO NEW LINES TO AN EXISTING AUDIENCE AND THREE NEW LINES TO A YOUNGER/OLDER AUDIENCE.

IF THIS IS THE CASE, HAVE YOU THOUGHT ABOUT WHERE THEY WILL SELL AND WHICH RETAILER YOU WILL BE TARGETING?

If by doing Game 04 you find that you have answers to all of the questions then you are most probably ready to get going with your production and begin selling your product to your end consumer. If you find you need more time to focus on this, continue to work back through this connect section and drive your sales forward through testing and getting prepared for your end consumers to buy into your product.

Either way, you are now ready to move on to communicate and look at how to engage your product and your brand with the outside world. This will allow you to think creatively about how people will engage with your brand and will also enable you to continue to think about the create and connect sections if you have not yet completed all of your tasks.

QUICK PEEK CHEAT SHEET

WHAT WE HAVE CONNECTED

BRANDFAMOUS.COM

01 FINDING A BUYER AND YOUR NICHE
DEFINE THE PRODUCT TO CREATE AND WHO TO
SELL IT TO (B2B AND B2C)

—

02 KNOWING YOUR PLACE IN THE RETAIL SPACE
SET YOUR OBJECTIVES AND CONNECT YOUR
PRODUCT TO RETAIL

—

03 BUILDING CONFIDENCE WHEN PRICING
GET RETAILER INSIGHT INTO YOUR COSTING
MODEL

—

04 GETTING READY TO PRODUCE YOUR PRODUCT
DECIDE HOW AND WHERE TO PRODUCE YOUR
PRODUCT

—

Enter your information at the school of brand fame to gain
more insight and also a game summary.
www.brandfamous.com/schoolofbrandfame

CHAPTER 07:
STEP FOUR #COMMUNICATE

CREATING CONVERSATIONS

Enter into the ... COMMUNICATE PHASE
My school reports from a young age always said, "Linzi could do a lot better if she stopped talking!" Little did they know I would make a career out of it...

Creating conversation: Getting seen, heard and spoken about
You have reached the point where you are now ready to get creative. You understand who you are and what you stand for, who you are talking to and what services you provide. Your toolkit and product vision have been created, so your message to the world is coherent with all your brand values and you have the tools to drive your business to the next level. This next phase looks at how to engage your customer so that they keep listening.

With some guidance from this chapter you will have the information you need to engage your brand with the five touchpoints you will learn about throughout the chapter. Each touchpoint will then create a huge spike in awareness for your brand. You will be provided with the tools, tricks and know-how to create a touchpoint storyboard (as discussed at the end of this chapter) that should enable you to realize how to engage your customers in a way that is impactful yet drives sales for

PAY ATTENTION TO YOUR FOUNDATIONS

the brand. In my opinion, this is the phase that brings the last four sections together to make the final difference with your brand ... providing, of course, you are well prepared in advance.

In my experience, nearly all businesses want to jump straight to this point. They want to decorate the house without paying attention to the foundations and continually just paint over the cracks every time they appear. These businesses tend to have a short-term lifecycle, launching products and services regularly while constantly refining things and contacting retailers without success ... mainly because the consumer, retailer or marketplace simply don't get it. Put simply, if you don't get it, how on earth will anyone else?

LINZIPEDIA: SHORT-TERM LIFECYCLE

—

A brand that struggles to take off and get noticed – it could just be a problem with a product line or worse still the entire brand.

It's time to get creative and let everybody know about your products, services and brand. It's time to land on the world stage with a bang. Imagine how it would feel if you could deliver a clear message that runs through everything you do: your services/products being adopted in your customers' lives. Your customers are regularly looking to your brand to re-engage with your product offerings over and over again through multiple platforms. You will be in a position to have conversation after conversation with readers who engage with every word you say and listen with a level of interest that engages them with the product or service offering that you provide, in effect pre-selling them into your brand making future sales easier for you. So, how do you create the possibility of engaging/re-engaging your customer on multiple platforms time and time again?

CREATING A SUCCESSFUL CONVERSATION

THE 360° TOUCHPOINTS APPROACH TO A NEW WAY OF COMMUNICATING

The old way of working was that you would have one idea and use one platform to speak to your audience. Growth was sometimes slow, especially without the aid of digital. Today, with all the technology available, any stand-out big brand should use the following five touchpoints for a single idea so that they can be heard through multiple channels. This is what I call your full communications offering:

01 TRADITIONAL PRINT (PRINT AND DIGITAL)

02 SOCIAL MEDIA AND DIGITAL ENGAGEMENT

03 BRAND PARTNERSHIPS/COLLABORATIONS

04 RETAIL ENGAGEMENT

05 EXPERIENTIAL EVENTS

It's important to acknowledge that this is not about trying to use just one or two of the touchpoints – all five are important and all must be included as part of your communications offering. Using only one of these touchpoints, which is what most brands will do, actually limits your communication potential. It minimizes communication to your target audience and you can easily be missed or ignored by many of your potential customers, regardless of whether you have defined who they are.

Now, consider how powerfully an idea can be executed when you are speaking to one person through multiple communication platforms, relaying the same message over and over again, always creating a different slant on the same idea so that your customer is constantly engaged and excited by your offering. Each touchpoint must be aligned to the relevant communication platform otherwise you will end up speaking to a totally different and disinterested target audience. Within your strategy, there should be a key touchpoint. This is the one that talks to your target audience whilst engaging with the other four touchpoints in order to maximize the message you are communicating. By engaging these five touchpoints in conjunction with each other, you will place yourself in a strong position that competitive brands will not have.

When setting objectives for your communications strategy you should think about the big vision which you intend to execute through the five touchpoints. Your business may be turning 10 years old this year, or you may want to launch in another country. You may need a strategy that engages with five big retail outlets so as to create an impact through your distribution channels. Perhaps you have changed your service offering or your target audience and you need to shout about it, or you want to engage with a new audience with a new line of products. For each big objective you set you must incorporate each of the five touchpoints so you can create a communications strategy that talks through each platform and has massive reach.

THE KEY TOUCHPOINT – EXPERIENTIAL

—

One of our Surgery clients, Desigual, wanted to increase their awareness in the UK. Desigual is quirky, unique and different and is always out to surprise. With this in mind, we needed to create and implement something that was different and unique to them.

The "semi-naked" concept was born with a creative campaign designed to let the world know that everyone who came to the Oxford Street store wearing nothing but their underwear would receive a free Desigual outfit. The communication strategy was written and the tools were created so that the target audience would be exposed to the idea before, during and after the event taking place.

LINZIPEDIA: EXCLUSIVE

—

Given to a publication so they are able to publicize the story before anyone else; this usually has an embargo attached to it, which means that there is a date set when they have to launch it and then everyone else can publicize
it afterwards.

LB SUGGESTS

Give yourself permission to get creative and think outside the box so that whatever idea you generate can be executed through the five touchpoints. Remember, the more touchpoints you speak through the more times you will be able to re-engage your target audience. The more times you get them to listen, the more chance you have of them buying in to your product.

01. TRADITIONAL PRINT

— Imagery and short e-alert created.
— Online and print media write about the upcoming event in an exclusive double page interview with Metro and Time Out to break the story before other publications.

02. SOCIAL MEDIA AND DIGITAL ENGAGEMENT

— Video viral created to promote the event.
— Online viral campaign run through Facebook and Twitter.
— Multiple bloggers tumble the image.
— Ripple effect created through blogging society.

03. BRAND PARTNERSHIPS/ COLLABORATIONS

— Partnered with Metro newspaper and Time Out magazine.
— Exclusive given to allow them to "break" the story before the event takes place (+ traditional print).

04. RETAIL ENGAGEMENT

— Event promoted through windows of Desigual stores nationwide.

05. EXPERIENTIAL EVENT

— Call to action for people to come in their underwear and stand outside the store; people got to experience the fun and playful side of the brand, which is one of their key messages.

The weather on the day was true British style, with a downpour of torrential rain – your worst nightmare for an agency promoting people to attend in nothing but their underwear. However, the event brought hundreds of people with a queue going all around the store on Regent Street with everyone stood in the rain in their underwear. A band from Germany had heard about the campaign on Facebook and flew into the UK to play outside the event for free in nothing but their underwear as well! After the event it was all over the Internet, in the national press and on the news. It created such hype that the stores saw a huge rise in sales both on the day and in the coming weeks, and an impressive increase in followers on Facebook and Twitter.

Did they raise their profile in the UK and have everyone talking about it? What do you think?
www.surgery-group.com

IN SUMMARY
—

EACH TOUCHPOINT CAN BE POWERFUL IN ISOLATION AND CAN PROVIDE YOU WITH A DEGREE OF SUCCESS.

USED TOGETHER, EXECUTING ONE IDEA THROUGH THE FIVE DIFFERENT PLATFORMS CREATES A DIRECTIONAL AND IMPACTFUL RIPPLE EFFECT THAT IS DESIGNED TO HELP YOU ACHIEVE STAND-OUT STATUS FOR YOUR MESSAGE.

NOW YOU HAVE SEEN THE TOUCHPOINTS IN ACTION, WE ARE GOING TO LOOK AT EACH ONE. WE DISCUSS THE FIVE TOUCHPOINTS AND HOW TO USE THEM ALL TOGETHER TO DEVELOP YOUR VERY OWN 360° COMMUNICATION STRATEGY.

PLAY THE TOUCHPOINT 01 TRADITIONAL PRINT DOT-TO-DOT GAME

INSTRUCTIONS

Read the dot, then play the game. Work your way through each chapter.

GAME
01

RESEARCHING THE RIGHT PUBLICATIONS FOR YOUR AUDIENCE

GAME 01
CREATE YOUR PRINT MAINTENANCE PROGRAMME

GAME 03

BECOMING FAMOUS IN
YOUR INDUSTRY ALONG
WITH THE BRAND

—

GAME 03
WORK OUT WHAT
#BRANDFAMOUS SHOULD
LOOK LIKE FOR YOU

GAME 02

CREATING SPIKES: GENERIC,
TAILORED AND BESPOKE
TO YOUR BUSINESS

—

GAME 02A
CREATE GENERIC AND
TAILORED SPIKES

GAME 02B
CREATE YOUR OWN BESPOKE
SPIKE

CHAPTER 08: TOUCHPOINT 1 TRADITIONAL PRINT

Print is now just one way of getting your message out. Ten years ago, this would have been the most important touchpoint to focus on, yet, as times have changed dramatically and are still changing, traditional print promotion is now just 15% of the pie when communicating your brand message. In 10 years' time, this is likely to change again as technology grows and our way of communicating with each other expands into more and more areas.

RESEARCHING THE RIGHT PUBLICATIONS FOR YOUR AUDIENCE

In order to speak to your target audience through print you must define the publications that they read. In your target audience profile you will have outlined a brief synopsis of what publications they read. Use this as a base to communicate on a print and digital platform by researching the magazine, relevant page and name of the journalists that you want to target.

The following game lists four key areas to help you find the best places to generate some traditional press. Think about who you are targeting, and what your client base and end customer read. You could send out a message on Facebook and ask your network to suggest what they read online and also in print – do they have favourite trade publications and are there articles that they are always drawn to?

LET THE DOT–TO–DOT BEGIN: COMMUNICATE YOUR BRAND

→ GAME 01
CREATE YOUR PRINT MAINTENANCE PROGRAMME

———

Under each of the following headings, list four publications and find the right person to contact. You will usually find contact details in the magazine or online. For example, if you work in health and fitness then look up the sports editor, the features editor for an article, the fashion editor for fashion and so on.

SOMEWHERE FOR YOU TO WRITE AN ARTICLE/COLUMN.

A PLACE FOR YOU TO BE AN EXPERT/ TALKING HEAD.

PAGES WHERE YOU CAN BE INTERVIEWED/ A FEATURE CAN BE WRITTEN.

PAGES WHERE YOU CAN HAVE PRODUCT PLACED.

This is a weekly thing to focus on in your business. It's how you maintain a constant presence in print media. These four areas for communication are the ones set in stone throughout your marketing plan. Things only change when the format of the magazine changes or the person within the publication is taken off the page and another person is allocated to write/edit the page.

Once you have been through the publications and drawn up a list of the four categories and where you are placed within them, you will then only need to re-evaluate the publications on a quarterly basis to see if any changes have been made.

Once you have created your wish list of publications, use the toolkit that you put together in the create section and send them a press pack of goodies that will entice them to you and your brand. If you want to write articles for the publications, then look through them for a number of months and figure out their style and what it is they write about. That way you can sell in a taster article and showcase your expertise in that field.

CREATING SPIKES: GENERIC, TAILORED AND BESPOKE TO YOUR BUSINESS

───

When putting your list of publications together you need to focus on certain times in the year when you could have a major spike in communications or want to focus your product to create a larger exposure.

LINZIPEDIA: SPIKE

───

A spike occurs at various points in the year, coinciding with your target audience's interest. In very plain English, ice-cream spikes in summer and Christmas trees spike in the month of December!

For different businesses there are very specific spikes to consider. If you aim to create the spike that engages your target audience, you will be in a position to maximize that period of time in the year and not miss out on easy sales. It is a great opportunity to get creative and try to infiltrate as many areas as possible – you are your brand. There are three levels of spike to consider.

01 Generic spikes

Generic spikes happen throughout the year and are based around:

— High summer – July/August.

— The big detox/health pages – January.

— Financial year end – April.

— Valentine's Day – February.

— Big events such as festivals, sporting events, Olympics, Royal engagements.

— The ski season.

These are all opportunities for you to engage with your audience in relation to an event that takes place at that particular time of year. There are also less obvious spikes to consider, such as National Happy Day, where we find less attention from a brand perspective and you will have more chance of your product featuring in the appropriate publication.

LB SUGGESTS
—

Do bear in mind that the bigger spikes like Valentine's Day and Christmas are inundated with people sending things to publications to get featured, so be creative and think outside the box where your product is concerned – hopefully it will get the attention it deserves and be featured.

When creating your calendar of spikes think about your products and services and where they fit into the year plan.

Timing and planning is everything – don't leave anything to chance!

What are the hot spots in your calendar seasons when you should get a product out? Once you have figured out the key spikes over the year to aim for, you should then start to look at tailoring them to your business.

If you are creative, you can think about providing services through a spike that on first impressions would not seem an obvious choice. For example, if you are a personal trainer your most obvious avenues for communication are sporting events and the January "get healthy" craze. But what about Valentine's Day? Don't be fooled into thinking that it is all about flowers and chocolates. A lot of pages these days are willing to promote anything and it is now a lot easier to grace those pages when you have something unusual and different to promote. Your personal training package can be repackaged to provide the same content with a different slant, to tailor it to the Valentine's season.

For example, say you decide to offer a "his and hers six-pack race" as the perfect treat for a couple to create their dream six-pack in six weeks whilst providing time to be together with "date hours" (exercising together) through the week. To create even more demand, tie this up with your online e-commerce store and turn it into a new product line to sell. Bundle the product with a partner product, for example a shopping experience at your most desirable retail store, where you can offer a discount for the client and an in-store personal shopper. This will for sure help your client show off their "new body" during a romantic evening with their partner: it's win:win! To promote a six-week programme for you and your partner whilst guaranteeing a dramatic transformation, what is more loving than that? Add in a marriage proposal at the end and your love is endless...

Christmas gift guides are major spikes in the calendar and national newspapers and glossy magazines dedicate their pages to promote products with a wide scope for all the family. You can think creatively about how to get your product featured on their pages by tailoring the product to suit. For example, you may be targeting women potty training their children. If you have designed a potty in your range, then repackage it so that you produce a limited edition range in specific colours exclusively for Christmas, sold through one department store and on your e-commerce site – what a perfect gift for mummy and baby!

LB SUGGESTS

TIMING IS EVERYTHING

when pitching your ideas. You must take into considera-
tion that publications have different timelines to produce
the content.

HIGH-PROFILE MAGAZINES

such as GQ, Vogue and Elle are long-lead consumer publications.
This means that if you are launching a product or want to be the
expert on a page of one of these titles, you must pitch this to the
publication three to four months before your launch date.

NATIONAL NEWSPAPERS

such as the Telegraph, Guardian and Sunday Times have lead
times of four to six weeks. You may find that the lead times
for the supplements inside them can be longer – sometimes up
to three months.

WEEKLIES

such as Now, More, Zoo and Nuts usually have a minimum
lead time of two weeks, since these publications are based
around having quick access to news, gossip and trends that
are changing rapidly.

DIGITAL ONLINE

where it was once always an instant sell in, has now become
more commercially minded and is often treated as a magazine
in terms of content and future planning. It is, however, still
classed as an instant hit as the lead times are shorter and
more accessible than going to print.

IT'S ALL A LOAD OF COBBLERS

I worked with a footwear company that had been trading comfortably for 10 years but was struggling with their distribution here in the UK. They had their own retail stores and a small wholesale business that were delivering average results with a product offering that was stable and slightly boring – black and brown shoes for men, nothing else. They were trying to sell to a retailer that bought hundreds of other footwear brands, but why buy their brand of black and brown shoes over someone else's?

They brought me on board to raise their profile in the UK and widen their distribution channel by 50%, targeting the likes of Selfridges, Offices and Kurt Geiger. In order for them to raise their profile and take a bigger slice of the retail space in the UK, we needed to redevelop their product offering. Money was an issue and retooling was expensive. We decided to use existing products in order to keep the expense down. We looked at the colourways that were being offered, which would involve a more cost-effective process than trying to build new soles and lasts, for example. We looked at what the catwalks were showing at the time for men and the luxury sector, and realized that some designer brands were looking at pastel colours to promote their ranges. This meant that the publication we needed to target would be showing pastels as their colours of the season. Although our footwear range was targeting the masses, we needed to have the product seen in all the key publications so it had a trickle effect down to the mainstream publications.

We chose to have styles that were very "of the moment" and changed the colours to produce them in pale pink, green and blue. This was in the early 1990s, when men were not ready to wear other colours. After the influx of colour in the 1980s, many men were still too afraid to experiment with it because it had been quite extreme – pastels were colour entry points for those afraid of the bright and garish prints of the previous decade.

We strategically chose the publications that were relevant for the shoes and created hype around the product. We offered the shoes as a limited edition product to Selfridges, which was one of their target retail outlets. We explained that we would take the stock back on "sale or return" if they did not sell. The last thing we wanted was any stock back, so we made sure that we established Selfridges as the main stockist – the primary place to buy them – as well as promoting the brand's own retail store. We then channelled all the editorial coverage to these two retail outlets.

We gained coverage initially in five key UK magazines, which created the desired buzz in their target audience to trickle down to the more mainstream magazines. Within weeks, both stores had sold out of these shoes. Not only that, but the sales of their brown and black shoes had also tripled due to the footfall that had been driven to the store and the attention that the brand was getting. Selfridges bought in to this shoe brand for all of their stores, which then acted as an exclusive window for other retail outlets to see – obviously they too would now want to buy in to the brand.

From this one project, the brand not only increased their circulation by 30% but also created a niche range of footwear that was low distribution in a variety of colourways other than black or brown. This created a new target audience who would buy in to the high-end product and, although it is low volume (e.g., not many retail stores are selling it), this drives awareness for the brand to go into new channels of distribution, leading to more sales of their existing styles which are sold through the now wider distribution channel.

The spike was already happening on the catwalks, pastel colourways were being introduced to men for the first time. We tapped into this spike to bring the shoe company up to date. We tapped into the existing product line of a company that had been trading for 10 years and looked at the trends that were taking place in the luxury sector that were not mainstream and could be utilized to enable the mainstream audience to take note without too much cost. It was a huge success.

GAME 02A
CREATE GENERIC
AND TAILORED SPIKES

—

Write down a list of generic spikes that happen throughout the year, which will enable your brand to create packages to engage with the press.

01 WHICH MONTHS ARE THEY IN?

02 WHAT IS THE CALENDAR OF EVENTS THAT COULD BE RELEVANT FOR YOUR BRAND?

03 WHAT PRODUCT PACKAGES ARE YOU GOING TO SELL INTO?

GAME 02B
CREATE YOUR
OWN BESPOKE SPIKE

———

Look at what trends/news is happening within your area of business. Think about how you can engage the press and retail to write about a certain product which you can create as an influencer, collaborative or limited edition line, whilst keeping the existing pattern which will create a ripple effect to then sell more product and open up your distribution.

WRITE DOWN ONE BESPOKE SPIKE AND THE FIVE STEPS THAT YOU WOULD NEED TO EXECUTE IT BOTH TO THE PRESS AND TO A RETAIL PARTNER.

LB SUGGESTS

———

Trend forecasting is a great way to think strategically about creating a bespoke spike. Most industries will have a trend forecast predicting what is going to be identified for the coming year – engaging with this information can allow you to think out of the box in terms of the product you are creating or how you would like to take your brand to market. For example, in the fashion and lifestyle world WGSN is a great source of information, as are publications like Elle Deco for interiors and high-end fashion magazines that release reports letting people see what is hot and what is not for the following season. Pantone also releases a trend forecast on colours, which is able to translate well into all different types of industry that can engage with the colours or pattern for their product creation to be noticed on different pages of magazines the following year.

BECOMING FAMOUS IN YOUR INDUSTRY ALONG WITH THE BRAND

Do you find yourself wishing that you had more time to ensure that you had great PR around you and your brand?

Are you always looking at your competitors and their achievements and wishing that you were having the same success as them?

Are you not being invited to the high-profile events or being asked to be a face of your industry?

If the answer is yes, then it's time to build your profile and brand superstar status. Be very clear about what you want your profile to look like and in which areas you want to be known.

As mentioned earlier in this book, you can achieve fame in your industry for the work, knowledge and industry insight that you are able to provide to a nation or better still on a global platform. Becoming a thought-provoking leader, a visionary entrepreneur, a globally renowned innovator or a market leader is now obtainable and ever more desirable with the entrepreneurial generation that has grown up in recent generations.

I work regularly with celebrities on turning them into a brand, which creates longer-term status and recognition than just having an initial outburst of fame. Your profile and status is an added thing that can give you and your brand superstar status. This is commonly overlooked and ignored, yet is an important area to focus on and one that is to be worked on daily.

01 Local

Look to the country that is your main channel for distributing your products/services. If this is your home turf it creates an easier transition to expand your profile by relying on the ease of your access and availability to you and your brand. It takes out the hassle of travelling to another country to create the promotion around the brand. You should maximize coverage in your country and make it a hot spot to focus on you and your brand. This can then work as a blueprint to propel you into the spotlight in other countries you want to venture into.

02 International

Look at the growth of your business and target the countries where you see natural expansion potential; use your profile to gain recognition in these countries. Set your objectives to be clear on how you wish to expand and in which countries. Before you step one foot into those countries, you should already have a profile. Your profile should be raised in those countries through talks, sales of books, websites and products so that when you arrive, people are already waiting for you – you need to be a known face in your field.

Set clear objectives for each country so that you are met with support and direction to react to the challenges presented in raising your profile overseas. You need to provide clear instructions so that your key message is being delivered whilst providing a long enough lead time so that the coverage pitched has time to be published before your product or service is sold to the market.

03 Digital

Raising your profile on a digital platform enables you to fast track the waiting game of lead times. With the press of a button your blog, interview, tweet or video can be recognized in an instant in multiple countries – make sure your profile is up to date and explains clearly who you are, what you do and ultimately what you want to be known for. Even if you are at the beginning of your career, you can speak your dreams into reality. You can infiltrate a country in a matter of seconds by targeting key online publications, podcasts, radio stations and video websites so that you can become #brandfamous with very little effort.

GAME 03
WORK OUT WHAT #BRANDFAMOUS
SHOULD LOOK LIKE FOR YOU

—

WRITE DOWN FIVE KEY POINTS FOR WHAT FAME
LOOKS LIKE TO YOU.

— It could be being asked to speak on your topic on a
   regular basis through different areas that complement
   your knowledge.

— You may have your own or be part of an expert panel
   on TV.

— You may have created your own TV channel that is
   watched by x amount of viewers.

— You may have written your own book that is sold globally
   and recognized as a must-have in your field of expertise.
At the end, write out what you would like to be: A market
leader, a thought provoker, a disrupter ...?

ONCE YOU HAVE PLAYED THIS GAME TAKE A LOOK AT THE NECESSARY STEPS THAT WILL MAKE EACH OF THESE THINGS HAPPEN; START BY UPDATING YOUR PROFILE ON ANY SOCIAL MEDIA SITES TO REFLECT WHO YOU ARE GOING TO GROW INTO.

CHAPTER 09: TOUCHPOINT 2 SOCIAL MEDIA AND DIGITAL ENGAGEMENT

Being online is your key to speaking to the world. Going global has never been so easy; using online platforms to reach out to the masses through viral and social media has made distribution in any country desirable and also achievable.

Expansion has never been as accessible or as lucrative as it is today. It's also possible to see which country is trending your product and which countries you are appealing to in the process. This makes the growth platform on an international level a lot smoother so that you can look to target countries in a more strategic way when you realize that a particular country is already providing you with a large amount of attention.

Digital PR and social media is the new age – a fast-twitch fibre that propels you to success when run in parallel with the four other touchpoints. The creative campaigns of digital PR and social media, coupled with how you want to talk to your target audience, should incorporate everything that you want to say to the world and as McDonald's would say, "do you want to supersize that, sir?" Your idea on a social platform will have a multiplier effect on any conversation that you have, taking a good idea into a great idea and one that is aired on a global scale rather than a local one. It speeds up the process without end.

CREATING DIGITAL CONTENT FOR ONLINE USE

Digital PR has been fully operating since 2005 and in the last five years it has created a wave of excitement throughout the media world. To my knowledge, we were one of the first lifestyle agencies at the time to introduce a digital division as a standalone area to be housed within the agency. We recognized very early on the demand for its inclusion, with a brand marketing plan based on the way the landscape for communication was changing.

PR agencies who have not transformed with the times have found themselves left behind as new-age PR took on board multi-platform communication strategies that incorporate digital PR as a given part of their print and PR strategies. Surgery now applies digital PR as the norm, as part of the basic PR package provided to a brand, and has transformed the digital division into Social Surgery which can execute a digital plan on all social platforms whilst incorporating the touchpoints into the mix and building communities.

YOU CAN HAVE INSTANT WINS WITH DIGITAL PR AS THERE ARE NO LEAD TIMES NEEDED IN ORDER TO GENERATE COVERAGE. TODAY, BLOGGERS ARE AS RECOGNIZABLE AS FASHION EDITORS OF VERY HIGH-PROFILE PUBLICATIONS AND ARE EVEN BEING USED AS THE FACE OF AD CAMPAIGNS. RECENTLY, BOTH H&M AND UNIQLO USED FASHION BLOGGERS TO MAKE A STATEMENT ON BILLBOARD CAMPAIGNS THAT WERE FEATURED THROUGHOUT ALL THE UNDERGROUND TUBE STATIONS IN LONDON. BLOGGERS ARE ALSO A PERMANENT FIXTURE ON THE FRONT ROWS OF CATWALK SHOWS AND ARE BEING TAKEN ON PRESS TRIPS SO THAT THEY WILL PROMOTE PEOPLE'S PRODUCTS ON THEIR ONLINE PAGES. ANYONE CAN BE A PART OF THE BLOGGER CREW; THE ONLY CRITERION NEEDED IS A HUGE FOLLOWING.

PLAY THE TOUCHPOINT 02 SOCIAL MEDIA AND DIGITAL ENGAGEMENT DOT-TO-DOT GAME

—

INSTRUCTIONS

—

Read the dot, then play the game. Work your way through each chapter.

GAME 01

CREATE CONTENT FOR YOUR DIGITAL PRESS

—

GAME 02

YOUR SOCIAL
MEDIA CHECKLIST
—

GAME 01
CREATE CONTENT
FOR YOUR DIGITAL PRESS

—

To achieve the maximum success rate, you need to be able to execute a digital PR campaign which has the following three tools to create hype around the product/brand you are promoting.

01 GREAT PRODUCT IMAGES SHOT IN AN INTERESTING WAY

This can create a tumble effect, so that your one image can get re-blogged to 100 different blogs over the course of 24 hours. The cost of that image may have been £100; however, in 24 hours that one shot could make you back 100 times the cost of producing it.

02 CONSTANTLY UPDATED VIDEO CONTENT SO THAT YOU IGNITE THE READER WITH INVALUABLE INFORMATION ON YOUR PRODUCT AND BRAND

There are three ways that video content can be formulated:

— Piece to camera – Giving tips on something that you have a voice of authority on.

— A conversation with – Interview someone who appeals to your target audience.

— A video of you showing something at work – 10 ways to create the best abs, or accounts made easy.

— Film an event and get video "vox pops" (talking heads) of key people within your industry talking about the event.

Video content is a great way to send a viral campaign out to bloggers and online publications whilst creating hype around the brand and taking ownership of your sector.

03 UP-TO-DATE NEWS

New news is key. Content creation for your digital network is critical. It is the main tool that you have to communicate your message to your fans in a visual language that is true to your brand values. So, when you create your content, create it well as it is your window to your audience and new potential fans.

Keep news short and to the point with great images attached – no one wants to read an essay. You will capture people's attention in five lines, so make sure that what you say makes the reader want more. Attach a strong image along with it and you will bring the news to life. Images are always easier to share – and more likely to be shared – than just text.

That is why platforms such as Instagram and Pinterest are so popular.

NOW WRITE YOUR PLAN HERE

GO SOCIAL → GO GLOBAL

When digital hit the scene in 2000, most people thought that Facebook, YouTube and MySpace were all for students to use; most people did not engage with the digital era and mocked it as something that would not catch on – something for the kids! Justin Bieber is a worldwide phenomenon who posted up a YouTube video of himself singing in his bedroom. He achieved vast numbers of followers and was blasted into the limelight from this one action alone.

Over the last three to five years, brands have started to engage with social media and realized that it is no longer about ploughing their marketing budgets into big advertising campaigns to generate success. Instead, brands can generate clever creative content, which can be used in a playful yet targeted way to talk to their audience and register with their consumers, and most importantly can be easily monitored. It is quantified through the number of hits and comments created, with genuine feedback being given straight from the horse's mouth.

Social media is still in its infancy, and looking forward to what's coming in the future makes this an exciting phase not to be missed. The worst decision you could make is not to jump on board now.

I AM GOING TO HIGHLIGHT THE DIFFERENT PLATFORMS YOU CAN USE TO CREATE A FOLLOWING OVERNIGHT THAT WILL FULFIL YOUR BRAND OBJECTIVES – HOW TO TURN YOUR BRAND GLOBAL INSTANTLY.

TOOLKIT REQUIREMENTS FOR YOUR SOCIAL MEDIA KIT

—

The importance of video, images and content

Without video and imagery you will find it difficult to get noticed. Video and image content is your key to successfully promoting yourself online. The better the content, the more stand-out you become. In this day and age it is easy and reasonably cheap to create great content. Using a socially connected camera or your smartphone to create video content can be just as effective as getting your shots taken professionally.

If you do have the resources to create a higher grade of imagery, there are plenty of freelance cameramen that also edit and will provide you with high-quality videos that you can use on your website or choice of social media page. They can also be used to send out as a viral campaign online to generate the hype that you need. Your aim is to take ownership of your virtual space on the Internet and be known as the expert in your field.

If the budget is tight then just ask around your colleagues and contacts – you might be surprised at what you find available. For example, when I was out in LA for our pop-up with Rankin's gallery, we had planned to create a mini film of the trip but our cameraman let us down. We literally placed an advert on LinkedIn for a camera person based in LA who was available to film and edit. Within three hours we had hired someone on the basis of their online showreel.

❝ ❞

—

If you want to make it happen, trust me you will. It is hard to get in the way of determination.

LB SUGGESTS

If you are camera shy there are other ways of filming your videos without you having to appear on camera. You can use someone else to front the campaign, use a voice-over person or interview people about your work. Images and graphical words can be edited into the piece, with other people talking about your business and its progression. The idea is that people understand what you do and engage in your projects and your brand without having to read lengthy text.

VIDEO

Based on who you are, your key message and your brand values, you should produce videos that speak your message to the world. The look and feel of everything you produce should be descriptive of your values. Your videos should be styled in a way that portrays the look and feel of your brand.

There are three types of video to create great content.

01   Credentials video (cred)

A three-minute credentials video, tastefully filmed, will talk about who you are and what you do, and incorporate the people you work with so they can provide you with video testimonials. This should be quick and easy to watch, so that it excites and entices the viewer, leaving them wanting more, with a simple call to action at the end. Your video testimonials can be past and present clients and/or people that have used your product. Anyone can be a spokesperson for you and your brand – get them to say how great you are and why your product works.

02   Testimonial video

This can be filmed at the same time as the credentials video and can be a more in-depth version of the mini testimonials shown there. You can then have them categorized – clients, students, journalists, opinion formers – it depends on your business. This is an area that can be updated on a regular basis, and you can send out a viral asking people to check out the new video launched. It is a great way to let new businesses know how great you are without you having to do the hard sell.

These are very short, 30–50 second videos in groups of five. Your aim should be to film approximately 30 of these videos so you have a bank of them that can be used to spike the Internet and the Google search engines. They can be done by one person speaking directly to the camera about your chosen subject in bite-sized chunks which are punchy and to the point. If you do not feel comfortable speaking to the camera, script it, use a member of staff or hire an actor to speak on your behalf. Don't miss out on the instant impact that these videos will have just because you are shy in front of the camera.

You can also film great content to be put into a box set. Think about your testimonials – do you have leading experts in your field that you can call on to have a conversation with? Is your business able to transform into a "How to ..." box set that people can buy on your website? Your box set can also become a book or an e-book, available online from your website.

ENGAGING IMAGES

❝ ❞

A picture paints a thousand words!

Frederick R. Barnard
National Advertising Manager 1920s

The easiest and most effective way of creating great pictures to be viewed in an exciting format at low cost is by using apps such as Hipstamatic or the ever-popular Instagram. Both of these can be used to create incredible images which can then be uploaded to Pinterest or Flickr and stored in a creative format whilst being able to be instantly shared with your social media community. By accessing these images you can create a great portfolio of all your work which documents your different events, workshops and launches. This makes it easier to combine your social media conversations in a simple way, for people to engage in and also for you to archive your work to create picture case studies with minimum text and maximum effect.

Upload your photos to your blog and social media pages to provide access to picture content. This is a great way for instant recognition and most people will press "Like" on a picture much more readily than when you write the same content in words. Remember the key to digital success: great content creates great coverage.

DO I REALLY NEED TO USE SOCIAL MEDIA?

Social media is only at the beginning and without the use of social media, your company will be overtaken by other businesses in the same field that are tweeting, blogging, posting on Facebook, uploading videos onto YouTube, Vimeo, Vine and posting slideshows on SlideShare. They will be embracing the new way of communicating with the world on a multi-platform approach that reinforces their message through word, video and slideshow content over and over again, not just on a local but on a global level. If you are not using social media wisely today, you will be going backwards not forwards.

At the time of writing this book there are key platforms that, between them, most people use: Facebook, LinkedIn, Twitter, YouTube, Vine and Tumblr. All are ways to create conversations with the outside world. However, in such a rapidly changing world I know this section will be outdated in the next three years, with new sites, new creative platforms and new ways of being online that will leave today's social media far behind. If one of your objectives is to raise sales over the next three years or increase your sales on a global level, then digital and social media are a great touchpoint to supersize your offering. Own your space and always remember who you want to talk to and why. Your target audience will dictate the content you produce, what you say, how you say it and where online you are most active.

WHY CREATE A FOLLOWING?

If you have a ready-made audience there will always be someone to talk to who will listen. They will tell their friends and it can go viral in the blink of an eye. I love when I take a photo and within a moment people outside my network are sharing it. It is better than any form of advertising, since every person you speak to is a ready-made listener; they are already engaged in what you have to say. You have never been able to speak to so many people in one go who are 100% there because they want to be and have even requested to follow you and hear what you have to say.

When you place an advert in a magazine or enter into a big billboard campaign you are talking to hundreds of thousands of people; however, only a small percentage of those are the people you want to engage. Using social media and creating a digital strategy enables you to speak to your target audience every single day.

ENGAGED PEOPLE

FUTURE CLIENTS

CREATIVE IDEAS AND IMPLEMENTING THEM SOCIALLY

—

When launching an idea online, with the goal of maximizing your reach, thinking creatively will have a huge impact on how many people are listening to you. If you create conversations with your listeners that engage them with something that they need, then they will not only listen but also engage with your brand instantly, becoming a potential customer for the future. Engaged people are future clients.

Why is creative content so important?
This kind of content can be executed through all of your touchpoints. Not thinking outside the box makes it more difficult to engage people in your brand. There are so many brands that want the same space as you. To stand out from the crowd, do something that is slightly alternative from what you would normally do and engage people in a way that is unique and individual. This makes it easier for you to get great PR online and in print, get the bloggers talking about you online and allow your social media to grow through likes and followers, creating an excitement that allows them to interact with your brand.

Telling is not selling

Don't tell them what you want them to know, allow them to experience it. The best execution of any creative idea is to allow the reader to engage in what you are telling them, to experience the idea and leave them wanting more and telling all their friends. If you can start the idea on Facebook and get people tweeting, blogging and following all the forms of social media then it sends a ripple effect of conversations that can be passed on numerous times from friend to friend until it goes full circle and someone comes back to you telling you that they heard about the great promotion that you did on the campaign for Desigual, for example. By utilizing the different social media platforms you can easily stand out with an extraordinary collection of YouTube videos that are cost-effective and easy to produce.

A SELECTION OF PLATFORM OPTIONS

Your options are endless; however, if you don't want to be socially obsessed and just engage on the platforms that are most relevant for your business then here are the most important ones currently available.

Facebook

Unless you have been living on another planet, I don't need to explain to you the benefits of Facebook. Why not upload a personal Facebook cover image unique to you and run a competition on the site?

Twitter

Build a rapid following and tweet to your heart's content using 140 characters or less. It's a powerful way of communicating and be aware that what you tweet can be seen by millions and spread like wildfire. Use your tweets to link out to videos, blogs and material that your followers will naturally engage with. Use hash tags, marry your content with what's trending locally or in the world and drive people to your twitter feed and get them into your content as soon as you can.

YouTube

On this video-hosting platform, you can create your own online TV channel to host all your videos and give you a unique point of difference from your competitors. Create exciting content and house it in a modern digital and easily accessible way. This will also up your profile on Google and help search engine optimization (SEO).

Vimeo

This is the place for B2B videos. It is known as the more high-end version of YouTube, where users browse for video content. Create exclusive video content with which you want to engage your audience to make them feel like they have access to content that is not readily available elsewhere.

LinkedIn

LinkedIn is a great business tool to connect with people in your industry and engage them in your product/brand. Unlike other platforms it enables you to speak with the MD of a business who would otherwise be impossible to engage with. It is underused in most businesses and the potential to open up new business opportunities and contacts is extreme. Make sure that your profile is current and lets people know exactly who you are and what you are up to in the world.

Google+

Rated the next big digital platform, Google+ is designed to overtake anything that Facebook is doing and is powered by the machine that is Google. Seeing is believing but, like any social media platform, to be seen, to get trending and to be shared worldwide your content must be engaging. Once Google+ takes off it will become a must-have, a bit like a Mulberry handbag. Try creating a hangout and engaging your followers face to face.

Pinterest and Instagram

Both are great ways of sharing images of events that you have hosted or talks, launches and workshops that you want your fans and followers to see. A must-have for anyone using picture content, which as I said previously is an integral part of your toolkit for great content online. Try tagging in people that you think will instantly engage with your content.

Klout

This is an addictive way of tracking your social influence, the higher your score the more influence and reach you have. It lets you know who you influence and who you are influenced by. Obviously the more people you influence and the less people you are influenced by, the more likely you are to be #brand-famous.

YOUR BOX OF DIGITAL TRICKS

———

Here is a list of everything you need in your digital toolkit to create great content:

PRODUCT IMAGERY — UPDATED REGULARLY.

LIFESTYLE IMAGERY — UPDATED REGULARLY.

VIDEO CONTENT, CREDENTIALS VIDEO, TESTIMONIALS, PIECE TO CAMERA.

GREAT PHOTOS — HIPSTOMATIC, INSTAGRAM/ VIDEO, VINE, CINEMAGRAM.

SEASONAL NEWS STORIES — CREATING CONTENT FOR ONLINE.

PRESS RELEASES.

STOCKIST INFORMATION.

UPDATED SOCIAL NETWORKS — MANAGED BY AND USED WITH YOUR TOOLKIT.

GAME 02
YOUR SOCIAL
MEDIA CHECKLIST

—

Have you been socially active today?
What have you created, written, filmed, photographed
to create a conversation with your audience?

FACEBOOK

TWITTER

INSTAGRAM

YOUTUBE

GOOGLE+

CHAPTER 10: TOUCHPOINT 3 BRAND PARTNERSHIPS/ COLLABORATIONS

COLLABORATION IS KING

Let me start by saying that if there is one thing you should do with your business, it is to look at collaborating with a person, brand, opinion former or celebrity that can really enhance or make a difference with the awareness of your brand. I have case study after case study documenting that one collaboration has literally repositioned somebody's business, spoken to a new target audience, created a distribution channel that otherwise would be impossible to get into and, in most cases, made the brand famous.

LB SUGGESTS

Visit www.surgery-group.com (search our work) and see how many times this has worked for some of your favourite brands (which have perhaps been brought back to exceed their former glory as a result of collaborating).

The most widespread comments that I hear when we suggest brands should collaborate are:

— "I am unsure who to collaborate with."

— "I am not aware of the benefits of collaboration."

— "I see my competitors collaborating and look at them with envy, wishing I had thought of it first."

— "I can't afford it."

— "I have tried collaborating in the past and it did not work."

COLLABORATIONS MADE EASY

The key to getting started is to first set your objectives in terms of what you want to achieve from a collaboration. This allows you to look at who will work with you and who you can work with to accelerate your brand to stand-out status. This can be in the shape of a well-known face or a brand that is strong in the marketplace, even someone that is not in your space. It might be someone who has a product you don't have, or it could be the service they offer – perhaps it's their fame or massive social media following – what's important is that it brings value to your brand and is on a par with your core values and key messages. Providing you have something that adds value to them as well, you have yourself a potential collaboration.

A very successful partnership saw Karl Lagerfeld, the head designer of Chanel, redesign the Diet Coke bottle. Everything has a fit, no matter what the product and collaboration might be – it just has to sit with your brand values and key message. Your first objective must always be the potential return on investment, what you want to get out of the collaboration and the reason for collaborating.

SIX TIPS FOR A SUCCESSFUL COLLABORATION

---

01. LOOK AT WHO TO PARTNER WITH TO GUARANTEE INCREASED DISTRIBUTION

To existing customers, or open up a new type of distribution channel that engages your existing and new target audiences identified in the earlier part of the process. The main aim of collaborating is to get more people talking and engaging with your brand.

---

02. INCREASE YOUR SOCIAL MEDIA EXPOSURE ONLINE

Through creatively leveraging the exposure of the person/brand you have collaborated with using behind-the-scenes exclusive interviews and imagery that can be released to online press and hosted on your YouTube TV channel. Monitor the levels of success through social data capture.

---

03. TIE THE PRODUCT IN TO YOUR COLLABORATION AND SELL MORE

Turn your collaboration into sales. You know this has worked when you get repeat orders – hopefully before the product has even hit the stores. Generate as much coverage as possible before the launch so that your stores have a waiting list. This really does happen, and I have evidence of this through many different brand stories.

---

04. INCREASE YOUR EXPOSURE TO CREATE THE SPOTLIGHT EFFECT

That comes from a great collaboration with a great brand. Engage journalists by being in the spotlight and get all the publications writing about you, both in print and online.

---

05. CREATE THE ELEMENT OF DESIRE SO THAT OTHER PEOPLE WANT TO COLLABORATE WITH YOU

This happens once you have a case study of success. When you go to that potential partner you want to collaborate with – the one you thought you would never even get to speak with – they may be readily open to have a conversation with you.

---

06. GET YOUR PRODUCT ON NEW PEOPLE AND IN NEW PLACES

Maximize your visibility to end consumers, who may not necessarily be engaged with your brand. This is optimal, as you will now have opened up a whole new cross-section of people wearing your product. You will notice this with your own eyes when you are sat in a pub, restaurant or bar and the cool kids are wearing your product.

HOW THE NEW-SCHOOL BRAND COLLABORATES

The old-school way of collaborating with a famous face was to employ a celebrity and use their face to sell the product. You will see this time and time again, used by many brands that are out their using collaborations in the marketplace; for instance, David Beckham and Armani. Content that engages people through brand and celebrity collaborations to supersize awareness of the brand in the marketplace through a non-traditional channel. Partnering up with someone who will add value to your brand is one thing, creating an experience for your customers to enjoy through the five touchpoints that communicate your message across multiple platforms is something else completely – and something that is only being achieved in a state of infancy at the moment.

Adverts need to lead to social media and social media need to lead to windows in retail stores, it is a magical trail of excitement that keeps turning up over and over again with the same face in different ways. Collaborations that endorse brands should be used as an extension of the brand to guarantee the end sale.

Think about the tools you can create to promote the collaboration; viral videos that link to YouTube channels or websites so as to drive traffic to your product/services and increase sales. Having a distribution outlet attached to the project increases the footfall of the consumer, guaranteeing sale after sale. The new way of partnering is to think about execution; the new age of successful brand collaboration thinks in a three-dimensional way. You certainly don't need to have the biggest budget, in fact many make the loudest noise without much money at all.

What they will all be doing is making sure that they execute the project so it is seen on multiple platforms, and have the tools in place to make this happen.

A TASTY LITTLE TECHY COLLABORATION

—

Fashion brand Burberry partnered with the iPhone 5 – prior to the official launch date – to capture stills, videos and celebrity snapshots at its prestigious London Fashion Week spring/summer show. It was a great example of fusing technology and fashion. They then went a step further and also posted a Vine – the latest social media fad of looping short video – of one of the creations being sketched out, which was also shot on the iPhone 5S. This created the desired effect that only such collaborations can achieve, with more press generated through print and digital than you could possibly imagine.

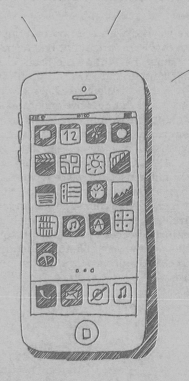

There are four different types of collaboration to achieve the success you want

01 Teaming up exceptional people linked to your brand
The goal of a partnership is for two partners, be they people or brands, to come together and create wider awareness in either an existing field or a new one. Partnerships are used widely in the fashion and consumer world, where collaborations take place with famous photographers, models, celebrities or opinion formers with the goal of raising the profile of the brand and creating a huge spike in following, in return hyping up the awareness of the photographer and/or celebrity collaborator. There is always mutual benefit to both parties, and each will achieve a huge increase in status, credibility and profit via a successful collaboration. This, however, will not be enough unless you have the missing ingredients to secure the coverage that raises the profile of the brand to achieve stand-out status.

SUPERGA AND ALEXA CHUNG

We worked with a brand call Superga, which is a niche Italian footwear range that had a small distribution channel and a limited following. The brand's objective was to increase its distribution and raise its profile in the marketplace so they could extend their reach to a wider audience of consumers. The brand did not have enough money to use Alexa Chung for an ad campaign, so we made her the face of their "in-store" campaign. This meant that Superga would not have the added expense of placing adverts in magazines, on buses and tubes.

Alexa Chung had an affiliation to the brand because her mum used to wear it when she was younger and had always loved it. We created a video viral of the shoot (www.surgery-group.com/superga) and used it to sell in as an exclusive video to Vogue.com, we then gave the Sunday Times Style exclusive access to both the photos and the interview with Alexa so they were able to publish the pictures before they were exposed on all the blogs, online publications and in the printed press.

THE BAROMETER OF BRAND FAME – SUPERGA

01.

Traditional print and digital PR
Within one month of releasing the pictures we had created over 1 million pounds' worth of coverage on this story alone, showcasing the same existing styles of shoe that were already in the collection. Within four months this had gone to nearly 6 million.

02.

Retail
The exposure from the campaign created such a buzz that they opened up retail stores with everyone from Office shoes to Selfridges and COS; approximately 150 retail doors in the UK.

03.

Celebrities championing them
Many different celebrities in both the USA and the UK are now seen wearing the shoes, talking about them and wanting to partner with the brand; they are the most desirable shoes, featured in many publications.

04.

Digital exposure
This was huge, with the Alexa Chung video that we filmed receiving over 50,000 hits – and that was on the official Superga video launch, not including all the other thousands who viewed the video on other platforms.

Although Alexa came with a price for the campaign, the return on investment for the brand was priceless as it way exceeded the key performance indicator set by Superga. They went on to do a second season using Alexa as their face, and created an exclusive shoe range with Henry Holland (Alexa's closest friend). They did not sit still either, from there they have moved on to Rita Ora – one of the hottest music artists in the UK at this time – and she has created the same huge impact that Alexa did the season before with a front page plus three-page interview in Metro newspaper that was "unpaid for" editorial coverage. They are a brand that understands this: In order to keep the brand moving forward, they need to stay ahead of the game so that they don't lose their status as a famous brand.

Always know why you are going into a collaboration with someone, what you want to get out of it and what your collaborative partner wants out of it too. It needs to be a win:win situation for both parties concerned, otherwise one or the other will not enter into the deal.

TASTEMAKERS AND CELEBRITIES

LINZIPEDIA: TASTEMAKER

Someone who influences us into buying/desiring a product by them being seen with it/wearing it.

There is a tastemaker, celebrity and influencer within every industry; there is always someone who will influence the minds of the people that you are talking to – you just need to pinpoint who they are and how you can gain access to them. It is a matter of having a can-do attitude and thinking creatively about how to approach these people. If you have something worth selling, then there are people interested in buying and trust me, it only takes one of these influencers to talk about your product/service to create a ripple effect for the whole of your business.

We are living in an age where friends and opinion formers influence what we buy and how we buy it. Social media, Trip Advisor and celebrities are a proven way of creating conversations where people can get free advice, listen to what others have got to say or look at how people are reacting to a brand. Why do you think the blogger community has been so successful and revolutionary for our time? It enables people to instantly create a conversation about a topic without time delay or tampering by magazine editors!

Creating a way for people who influence your target audience to be seen wearing your brand, writing about your brand and creating conversations around your brand – positively endorsing your product – guarantees increased awareness and sales of your product/service and creates a route for the online industry to talk about your product in a positive light.

Surgery has worked with Wrangler jeans for a number of years and when Jamie Oliver walked out of the hospital with his new baby girl, and David Beckham stepped off a plane wearing "double denim" – a denim jacket and shirt from the Wrangler collection – both were captured and featured instantly in the press. This created a flurry of conversation about the Wrangler brand that would generate 2 million pounds' worth of coverage alone. The repercussions of this are simple: the brand sells out in their retail stores, reorders, and new distribution channels are opened with retailers desperate to get hold of the brand.

Tastemakers and opinion formers can have the same impact as a celebrity on your product. Your target audience may be mainstream; however, by targeting the tastemakers/influencers they then influence your mainstream consumer and get them to look out for what the influencer is wearing, using and where they can be seen. Ultimately, this creates a following for the brands at a grass roots level.

02 Packing up products and services

A cross-collaboration is where you can partner with other people's products to enable two non-conflicting brands to create a bigger offering of your service or product.

Let's say you work with new mums. You might be a nutritionist. You could combine your nutritional package with a personal trainer's five-session package and offer a food box delivered to their house each week. You could set an incentive where, once they have achieved their weight loss goals, they then get a personal shopper for a day with a discount at a high-street store.

There are great ways of teaming up with multiple services to provide an incredible package to enhance your brand offering. This could then generate a huge amount of press coverage if the project was given a name and teamed up with a retail store. You could offer this package to five journalists to experience it and two celebrities to write about the great package and the results it has created. Are you thinking that this all sounds great but you don't have any of the contacts to make it happen?

03 Brand-to-brand partnerships

If you want to infiltrate a distribution channel or appeal to a different target audience, this is a great way of being able to do it. Your brand might be very high end and you want to sell more products through a mainstream market without damaging the credibility of your brand. You will see high-end designers partner with mainstream retail stores such as Top Shop, New Look and H&M to create a desirable product for a mass-market customer. You will also see mainstream brands such as Fred Perry partner with very high-end niche brands such as Comme Des Garcons to elevate the level of exposure for both brands; putting the two together does not damage the name of either brand. It enables people to buy in to Comme Des Garcons who otherwise would not be able to afford it and in return, Fred Perry have their position elevated to sit in a more exclusive area and speak to influencers rather than mainstream people. Neither one of these has their own positioning in the market affected, since they are partnered with a brand that adds value to theirs.

04 Joint ventures (JV) and partnerships
You may have a product that would complement someone else's and yet you do not have their extensive database of contacts within which to infiltrate the marketplace. Why not look at a JV or allow them to white label your product.

Engaging with any of these four types of collaboration/ partnership could open you up to a whole new market that you would not have previously considered possible. Yes, you may need to go in at a 70/30 split, but is it not better to give away a small amount of your sales revenue to access an area that you otherwise would not be able to? I am a big believer in partnership with experts in fields that complement yours but do not conflict in any way. We have recently teamed up with a fabulous PR agency that works on restaurant, travel and TV PR; also an e-commerce app-building company so that we can sell all the products on the TV channel and also on an app and then sell this process to all the brands that we are working with. Both parties concerned are excited about this partnership as they will be able to upsell their own product by putting it into a package with another complementary partner; it makes them look at a bigger offering, so enabling them to play and win at a bigger game and allowing them to make money in an area they have no expertise in and grow their brand to a new target audience.

THINK AGAIN!

That was my biggest motto in life from a very young age, and how I drove everything in business – I never thought that anyone was unapproachable nor did I believe that they would not work with me; why wouldn't they? And if I did get a "no" then I pushed on until I got a "yes", sometimes not letting go of the original person until they finally changed their mind. There is talent and there is determination and one can go hand in hand with the other; however, you don't need great talent to become the best you just need a strong will to succeed.

PLAY THE TOUCHPOINT 3 BRAND PARTNERSHIPS/ COLLABORATIONS DOT-TO-DOT GAME

—

INSTRUCTIONS

—

Read the dot, then play the game. Work your way through each chapter.

GAME

01

COMMIT TO THREE
COLLABORATIONS/
PARTNERSHIPS IN THE
NEXT SIX MONTHS

—

01 JOINT VENTURE

02 BUSINESS BUNDLE

03 INFLUENCER PERSON

TIM FERRISS IN *THE 4-HOUR BODY* TALKS ABOUT REJECTION AND PROMOTES A MOVEMENT CALLED "FAIL BETTER" — I READ THIS AND LEAPT WITH JOY. IT IS EXACTLY WHAT I TEACH MY STAFF AND WHAT I WILL INSTIL IN MY KIDS AS THEY ARE GROWING UP. AIM HIGH, AND LEARN HOW TO DEAL WITH REJECTION. CONTACT THE PEOPLE THAT YOU THINK ARE UNREACHABLE AND PUT YOURSELF OUT THERE TO REALLY CONNECT WITH THEM. CONTACT THEM INITIALLY WITH NO MOTIVE TO SELL TO THEM OR GET ANYTHING FROM THEM — NOT IN THE EARLY STAGES ANYWAY. YOUR ONE AND ONLY GOAL SHOULD BE TO TALK TO THEM AND BEFRIEND THEM. THAT WAY, YOU WILL BUILD UP THE MILLIONAIRE DATABASE THAT WILL ONE DAY BE PRICELESS.

NEVER ALLOW REJECTION TO STOP YOU FROM CREATING PARTNERSHIPS.

GAME 01
COMMIT TO THREE COLLABORATIONS/ PARTNERSHIPS IN THE NEXT SIX MONTHS

—

ONE THAT YOU CAN JOINT VENTURE WITH THAT WILL MAKE A CONSIDERABLE DIFFERENCE TO YOUR BUSINESS.

ONE BUSINESS THAT YOU CAN BUNDLE UP WITH SO THAT YOU ARE ABLE TO SELL YOUR PRODUCT FOR A HIGHER PRICE.

ONE KEY PERSON WHO WILL ENHANCE YOUR BUSINESS BY PROMOTING YOUR PRODUCT – THE GOAL IS TO SERIOUSLY SPIKE THE AWARENESS OF YOUR BRAND IN THE MARKETPLACE.

Commit to contacting one person per month whom you class as unreachable and don't take rejection. Aim to get their personal email address and engage them in a conversation, asking them a meaningful question that will open up a dialogue. The aim is to maintain email contact and befriend them so you can start to work with them in some kind of collaborative way in the future.

Collaborations and partnerships can be the single most important way for you to get your product seen and heard about on a huge scale, without which access to these markets will take forever and in some cases may never happen. You just need to be clever about whom you are partnering with and what return on investment you will get out of the deal, so that it is beneficial to both parties. There always has to be a win:win with everything that you do when you are working alongside another person or brand.

CHAPTER 11: TOUCHPOINT 4 RETAIL ENGAGEMENT

You may be wondering why retail is one of the touchpoints and why this is so important in successfully turning your brand famous. A retail partner is not necessarily someone with a store on the high street. It can be a partner on the Internet, a chain of gyms, a restaurant chain, nightclubs, book stores, etc. The only thing that all of these have in common is that they are able to promote you and sell your product to your target audience.

My suggestion is to choose or focus on a flagship store or a key distribution partner to create awareness around your brand. This enables you, critically, to maximize your exposure and ensure further distribution through other retailers. I have listed below the six-step process to being able to create awareness around your brand with a retailer.

01 Choose the retail partner/distribution channel that will guarantee maximum exposure for the brand – make sure that the retailer you choose is high profile and will ensure you gain maximum coverage as a result of partnering with them.

02 Align your brand with a partner that is already speaking to your target audience – there is nothing worse than thinking that your product should be for sale in a particular store and you don't sell any product simply because their target audience is not aligned with yours. You need to do your research on this before you even contact potential partners (as discussed in the connect section). Google their brand, call up their office, do your market research if you have to but just make sure they are aligned with your brand.

03 Find the best person, using your five degrees of separation, who has the contact to get you into the distribution channel you need. Give them an introductory fee so that they are happy to open the door and you get seen without having to cold call – which rarely works. It can be a case of who you know not what you know... and if you don't know them, who does?

04 Think about a creative way of approaching the retailer. Would you like to send them an iPad with a three-minute film of your business preloaded onto it? What packaging could you use to show your product so that it stands out from the crowd? Is there an event that you could invite them to that would showcase what you do in a dynamic way? Be sure to make a statement rather than just contact them in the normal way. Leave a lasting impression on the person being contacted. A cold call never works.

05 If you want to sell through a retail store/partner and you are struggling to get a meeting or perhaps they have turned your product down in the past, think about creating an exclusive product line/range with a creative campaign attached to it that is aligned with their key message and core values, enabling you to sell your product through that store. Another option is to find a desirable partner to entice them to buy in to your limited edition range so that it enables you to get that foot in the door.

06 Once you have sold in to the store make sure that both parties are working on the market entry strategy. Create a concept that will sell product and up the profile of your brand so that it guarantees product sales and enables them to provide you with repeat business for the following season or for them to then buy in to your main collection.

HOW TO ENTER INTO YOUR SELECTED DISTRIBUTION CHANNEL USING A BRAND-TO-BRAND PARTNERSHIP

Brand-to-brand partnerships are an incredibly effective way of infiltrating a new audience or a distribution channel. A popular way is for a large mainstream brand to collaborate with a high-end designer or luxury brand. This creates huge awareness in the marketplace you are looking to infiltrate and raises your brand's profile to the tastemakers and opinion formers that dictate what we do and how we do it.

PLAY THE TOUCHPOINT 4 RETAIL ENGAGEMENT DOT-TO-DOT GAME

—

INSTRUCTIONS
—

Read the dot, then play the game. Work your way through each chapter.

GAME

01

SET UP YOUR
RETAIL PARTNERSHIP

—

01 RETAIL PARTNERSHIP

02 5° OF SEPARATION

03 CREATIVE APPROACH

04 IN-STORE EXPERIENCE

THE BIRTH OF
ALDO RISE

Recently, Aldo collaborated with five high-end designers to create a limited edition collection called "Aldo Rise". Aldo is a well-known shoe range that raised its profile by making the association with these desirable labels. They not only saw a 20% rise in press coverage through high-end publications, both online and in print, but the shoes were also being worn all over the globe by A-list celebrities and journalists on the front row of all the catwalk shows.

Aldo's biggest win was to create a joint venture with Selfridges; Selfridges was earmarked as a store that had a high priority distribution tag attached to it as one of their key objectives. The main objective for Aldo was to raise the profile of the brand and create a joint venture with Selfridges. Selfridges gave Aldo a double window during Fashion Week which was the seal of approval from the store that acted as a ripple effect to the end consumer. Selfridges was allowed to sell Aldo Rise exclusively for one month before selling the shoes nationwide through Aldo only stores.

From creating this one project they are now looking to partner with Selfridges on their core collection and open up a "shop in shop" (Aldo's own branded shop) through all of the Selfridges stores nationwide.

www.surgery-group.com/Aldorise

CREATING RETAIL PARTNER SUCCESS

If you are fortunate enough to already be selling to a retail partner then how can you guarantee the sell-through and the product awareness to raise the profile of the brand? A lot of people make the mistake of thinking that selling the product in to a store is enough and the store will sell out just by default. This creates problems for brands when the store ends up having excess stock and has to sale the product at the end of the season and fails to reorder the following season. Not good... You lose your distribution channel, exposure and, ultimately, income. Without your retail support you are missing the key ingredient to make this a success. However, there are three ways that should be part of your distribution strategy so you can open up your product, through effective simultaneous channels, to create the awareness for the brand.

01 Create your own retail outlet using an online store
This enables you to always have a place to direct customers to. Any publication that is going to give you press expects that you are able to sell your product to the UK audience and not just a London one. It also creates a permanent place where you will always be able to promote and sell your products. Excess stock can also be sold through an online store; you can also control the pricing, maintaining control of such problems as marked down prices that so often happen when a retail store cannot sell your stock. For example, having an online store means you could buy your stock back from a retailer who wants to discount it. The last thing you want is for your retail partner to sell it on to a discounted downmarket store that could ruin your brand.

02 Create a temporary space known as a pop-up store
A temporary "pop-up shop" is a place you literally pop up in. It is an empty retail space with a short let, which could even be as short as a week. It's a place where you grab people's attention, open a door for them to walk in, display and sell your products – the goal is to get them to buy your product and ultimately to buy in to your brand. A pop-up is a place where you can create an experience to bring your product to life. I worked with an underwear range that was selling in all the top luxury retail stores. They wanted to generate some press to drive traffic to their online shop. The brand created a pop-up store. The store was open for one week only and had an ice-cream van parked outside with the ladies, dressed in underwear, serving from the van.

Thanks to the promotion of this pop-up space, their online store became very busy, very quickly and it provided us with a story to promote the brand. We simply promoted their online store by talking about the pop-up retail event that had been created for just one week.

03 Create an in-store experience

Partnering with a flagship retail store or distribution partner creates exposure and kudos around your brand so that you can promote your product, drive sales and increase the profile of your brand, in turn increasing your distribution network. When you get into your desired retail store, set up or create an in-store experience that your customers can try. An in-store experience brings the product that you are trying to sell to life and also enables the customer to appreciate what it is your brand is about and why you are selling in that particular outlet. It's a great opportunity to attract press, generate social media campaigns and, again, generate customer awareness. Any experience you create always has to be on brand and relevant to what you are trying to say.

I have always found that having all three of the above as a collective force is the best method to create the strongest launch platform for your brand. This will give you your own online retail store to drive traffic to, coupled with the use of a pop-up store to get creative in, and an experience to showcase your brand that can either be run alongside your distribution partner or in a standalone venue if you are unable to partner with a store.

Once you have created the hype about your brand, then you can think about your second tier of distribution; creating a network of stores/channels around the country or even the globe. These enable you to sell your product to like-minded stores nationwide. This, in turn, widens your product to be seen and bought through many retailers and grows your brand to become widespread within the marketplace.

Many big brands use the influencer/mainstream mechanism to enable them to infiltrate two types of target audience at the same time and they always use their distribution channel to make this happen. Let me give you an example of one of my clients who recently did this.

SET UP YOUR
RETAIL PARTNERSHIP

—

Here is a list of things that you can go through to make sure that you are ready to get your retail partnership set up and engage with your brand:

WHICH PRODUCT LINES HAVE YOU PRODUCED THAT YOU CAN PUT A CREATIVE SPIN ON/ CREATE A PARTNERSHIP WITH THAT WILL ENABLE YOU TO PARTNER WITH A KEY RETAILER?

MAP OUT YOUR FIVE DEGREES OF SEPARATION FROM MAKING THAT CONTACT WITH RETAIL — MAKE SURE YOU GET THE PERSONAL CONTACT.

DON'T COLD CALL. WHAT IS YOUR CREATIVE APPROACH TO THE RETAILER THAT WILL MAKE YOU STAND OUT FROM THE CROWD?

DON'T ALLOW THE PRODUCT TO SELL ITSELF. WHAT CREATIVE EXPERIENCE IN-STORE CAN YOU COME UP WITH TO DRIVE TRAFFIC TO YOUR PRODUCT AND PR IT THROUGH YOUR MULTIPLE CHANNELS?

THINK ABOUT A CREATIVE POP-UP STORE ON YOUR OWN OR WITH YOUR RETAIL PARTNER TO ALLOW PEOPLE TO HAVE AN EXPERIENCE OF YOUR BRAND. WHAT WOULD THIS LOOK LIKE?

Finally, fail better. If at first you don't succeed, try, try again until you do. Successful people don't take "no" for an answer.

SUITS YOU

Superdry is already brand famous and definitely has a stand-out status of its own. They were keen to maintain their core business but also to infiltrate those customers that might not ordinarily want to shop in Superdry stores. They decided to partner up with a very high-end and niche tailor called Timothy Everest. They wanted to appeal to the 5% influencer audience so that they could communicate with them and have them re-engage with the brand.

Timothy Everest is very credible within the small circle of people who could potentially influence Superdry's existing customer. This enabled Superdry to create a lot of press around the brand, with double-page editorial spreads in Metro and GQ. They also saw a huge uplift in online coverage, which re-engaged them with their influencer audience by being talked about in the press to keep the brand at the forefront of people's minds.

This Superdry product was sold through limited distribution with a high-end exclusive event taking place in their flagship store on Oxford Street. A minimal amount of product was produced, so that it kept the collaboration exclusive and elite.

I mentioned in the opening chapters of this book the importance of high-end and mainstream, and that stand-out brands use both to infiltrate a marketplace. This would never be possible without the support of a distribution channel to make it happen.

THE NEWS

SUPERDRY X
TIMOTHY EVEREST

CHAPTER 12: TOUCHPOINT 5 EXPERIENTIAL EVENTS

Creating an experience to allow people to truly embrace your brand is as important as your branding, marketing, product and distribution. Without creating the experience, no one can truly engage with the essence of your brand and know what it feels like to really experience what you're about. There are many brands that stay one-dimensional, going for straight-up PR or expecting that their social media will do all the work of spreading the word. Without creating an experience, your campaign may only hit 70% of its potential. The best creative campaigns that I have worked on have always been well received when there was an experience attached to them. By utilizing this knowledge you should be able to create projects that captivate audiences, engaging and igniting them with your brand and having customers realize its huge potential via creative brand experiences.

Are you wondering how this crosses over to your line of work?

Although my agency started in the fashion and lifestyle sector, we now work with a multitude of different businesses across all sectors that require an experience for their customers to both enjoy and better understand the brand rather than just reading about it in an article or on a website.

How do you feel when you have been to a concert and watched an artist perform live – you go straight out and buy his album, right? When you have been on a day workshop with a yoga instructor who has made it possible for you to touch your toes for the first time in 20 years – you buy her DVD or book, don't you? Imagine just reading about the artist, or inspirational yoga teacher. You might look them up online but not necessarily purchase a product. Experiences get your client one step closer to purchase. Make sense? On some level, if you create an experience that is accessible for your target audience to get involved in, they will be more willing to become a loyal follower of your brand. You can create these experiences for small target groups such as buyers, journalists or people joining a course that you are promoting... basically, any audience or market you can think of where you want to sell your product.

"How can I do this for my business?" I hear you ask... Well, the main thing I will say is that everything has to link back to your key message and core values, which we touched on at the beginning of this book. When you link this to your experiences, whatever experience you create will always stay in line with who you are and what you stand for, and that carries your brand message further and stronger than anything.

PLAY THE TOUCHPOINT 5 EXPERIENTIAL EVENTS DOT-TO-DOT GAME

INSTRUCTIONS

—

Read the dot, then play the game. Work your way through each chapter.

GAME

01A

CREATE WHAT YOUR EXPERIENCE LOOKS LIKE

—

GAME **02**

**CREATE YOUR
TOUCHPOINT
STORYBOARD**

—

GAME **01B**

NUTS AND BOLTS

—

GAME 01A
CREATE WHAT YOUR EXPERIENCE LOOKS LIKE

—

How can you create what your experience looks like whilst tying in to the other four touchpoints?

01 WHAT IS THE ONE THING THAT YOU ARE TRYING TO ACHIEVE IN THE NEXT SIX MONTHS? THIS COULD BE TO INCREASE YOUR TURNOVER BY 25%, RAISE AWARENESS OF YOUR BRAND AROUND THE UK OR GENERATE GREATER INTEREST IN A PARTICULAR PRODUCT LINE.

02 ONCE YOU HAVE DEFINED YOUR BIG GOAL, LOOK AT WHAT IT IS AND WHERE IT COULD BE LAUNCHED FOR MAXIMUM EXPOSURE – IS IT ONLY IN YOUR MAJOR CITY OR THROUGH MULTIPLE CITIES OR ALL OVER THE UK? WOULD YOU ALSO LIKE TO HIT PEOPLE IN OTHER COUNTRIES?

03 GET FIVE TO TEN CREATIVE PEOPLE IN A ROOM WHO WORK ON YOUR BRAND TO BRAINSTORM WHAT A CREATIVE CONCEPT MAY LOOK LIKE. IT HAS TO BE SOMETHING YOU CAN ACHIEVE.

04 WORK OUT THE TEAM TO CREATE THE PROCESS; WHAT ARE THEIR ROLES AND RESPONSIBILITIES?

05 WRITE OUT A TIME LINE WITH A COSTING ATTACHED ALONG WITH THE INITIALS OF WHO IS GOING TO ACTION EACH JOB AND WHEN, SO THAT THE PROCESS RUNS SMOOTHLY. ALLOW NO LONGER THAN SIX MONTHS TO GO TO LAUNCH. DOWNLOAD THE GANTT CHART FROM #BRANDFAMOUS/GANTT CHART.

06 WRITE A LIST OF THE PARTNERS RELEVANT TO MAKING THIS EXPERIENCE COME TO LIFE. ALONG WITH THE DISTRIBUTION PARTNER AND/ OR A POP-UP SPACE TO SELL IT FROM.

MOVE?
REMEMBER FROM TOUCHPOINT 04 THAT YOU ARE ABLE TO CREATE A POP-UP SPACE TO HOUSE YOUR EXPERIENCE SO THAT YOU CAN HAVE THE FREEDOM TO TAKE ON A SPACE IF YOU ARE UNABLE TO CREATE A PARTNERSHIP OR SELL YOUR PRODUCT WITH A RETAILER OR DISTRIBUTION CHANNEL.

LB SUGGESTS

Search for a pop-up space that is on brand for you. If you are looking for an actual shop then contact estate agents with free spaces and see if they will rent to you for a week/month as required.

So now you have the nuts and bolts, let me help you get creative. People always overthink the situation, when it needs to be logical and not too complicated so that your customer will buy in to it and leave wanting more. What you need to be very clear on is that you can create any experience and execute it in such a way that it gets people to sit up and take notice of what you are doing whilst engaging with your brand and its values. Here are examples of two types of business, one product and one service, engaging with their customers in an experiential way.

GAME 01B
NUTS AND BOLTS

Once you have the first six points in place, the next four are the nuts and bolts to make the process happen.

01 WHO IS GOING TO PROMOTE THE EXPERIENCE?

Will you use a PR agency for the project or employ a freelance PR person? Either way, you need to set clear objectives for the results you expect. Find out what experience they have in digital PR and creating an online campaign. Create the PR hook – something that enables you to sell the concept as a news story both online and in print.

02 HOW WILL YOU CREATE THE EXPERIENCE AS A SOCIAL MEDIA CAMPAIGN AND CREATE VIDEOS TO SEND OUT VIRALLY BASED ON THE CREATIVE CONCEPT?

03 WHICH PRODUCTS WILL YOU TIE IN TO THE EXPERIENCE TO SELL THROUGH A DISTRIBUTION CHANNEL/POP-UP SPACE OR BOTH?

04 ARE THERE ANY PARTNERS YOU WILL COLLABORATE WITH TO ENABLE YOUR RETAIL PARTNERSHIP TO SUCCEED?

TEA COMPANY —
TOUCHPOINT STORYBOARD

A lady I know is importing tea into this country and wants
to be the go-to person for the different types of tea that
she sells.

RETAIL ENGAGEMENT (TOUCHPOINT 04)

Her experience can be a pop-up teashop in central London
where she rents a retail space for a month and opens up a
teashop fusing the worlds of tea – bringing in different types
of tea, with different ladies serving their regional type of tea
and providing lessons on the benefits of that tea as opposed to
the others.

DIGITAL/SOCIAL MEDIA (TOUCHPOINT 02)

She can sell her different selections of tea online, with videos
attached to each one explaining what the benefits are for a
Japanese, Asian or English tea and how to make it, and then
direct customers straight to her website to buy the teas – using the e-commerce site beautifully.

  She can create a "Time for Tea" YouTube TV channel
which explores and interviews people on their taste in tea and
when the most suitable time for tea is. She can then use this as
a viral campaign on her social media site – even better if she
can interview some famous faces on their particular taste in
tea using her five degrees of separation.

COLLABORATION (TOUCHPOINT 03)

To get great PR on the pop-up store, she could team up with
three prominent designers from different countries and
get them to create the packaging for the tea from their re-
gion. This creates a unique talking point and easily com-
plements social media, adding to the experience in-store.
Each designer could also provide a uniform to be worn
in-store, which can also be sold along with their limited edition tea boxes on the e-commerce site and in selected stores
nationwide.

EXPERIENCE (TOUCHPOINT 05)

She can have "Time for Tea" afternoons for yummy mummies to experience afternoon tea with their babies and run the "Time for Tea" YouTube channel at the same time, to interview, run videos and show master classes that will teach people about tea. These can then be used as a viral campaign on social media to tease people to watch the "Time for Tea" channel... and drink more lovely tea bought from her online store.

She could run a social media campaign where people can use a hash tag such as #teattime and ask people to tweet about their favourite time and type of tea. She could have a tweet board in the shop that shows all the different tweets as they get posted in real time.

PRESS/DIGITAL AND PRINT (TOUCHPOINT 01)

The YouTube channel, print media, online press and blogs will drive traffic and sales to sell the product, with the pop-up store experience creating a news story for the journalists to write about.

She could then host an event for journalists, influencers and bloggers to launch the limited edition designer teas, with the designers themselves acting as hosts for the evening; thus guaranteeing PR for the pop-up teashop, PR on the designer collaboration and a great profile build for the lady who wants to be known for her tea.

Did this go around all the five touchpoints and create an experience for people to understand and also leave them wanting more? I think so...

You might be thinking that it's easier to be creative about a lady who has a product over your deathly boring service... My answer is that there is always room to create an experience, whether you are selling a product or a service. You will inevitably end up creating products by the default of being exceptional at what you do.

THE CREATIVE ACCOUNTANT STORYBOARD

———

Just in case you really doubt that this sequence will work for any business, I am going to give you an example of how the five touchpoints work for an accountant who specializes in helping small businesses with their financial structure and tax management.

His target audience is a 20–35 entrepeneur. He has no product at this point, only services to sell.

One way to enable him to do this, for example, is to create a set of podcasts: "How to grow your business from the inside out", with the goal of educating a young entrepreneur in business, whilst establishing the accountant as a face for the young setting out on their journey into the world of self-employed finance.

DIGITAL/SOCIAL MEDIA (TOUCHPOINT 02)

Once the accountant has his message in a sellable product (DVD or podcast), the rest will follow via three ways he can promote himself and engage with his target audience:

— Set up an e-commerce site in conjunction with his website. He can then sell the box set and create e-books to sell on his own site, making maximum return on his investment.

— Create downloadable videos no more than 30 seconds long, hosted on his YouTube TV channel and posted on his social media, offering information on the types of mistake people make when setting up in business and the things that must be considered when presenting a cash flow to the bank. Get the picture? What information does your target audience need?

— Make a 3-minute video based on himself: who he is, his credibility, what he is trying to achieve in his business, how he can help you in a way nobody else can and an outline of how simple it is to begin working him today.

RETAIL ENGAGEMENT (TOUCHPOINT 03)

There are three distribution channels that the accountant could have, not taking into account his own e-commerce site which should be a given:

— His main retail partner could be QVC, as this is the perfect place to sell high volume and enable him to be interviewed about his product for a wide audience, thus upping his profile with a mainstream audience.

— An affiliate programme – selling through his clients' websites and giving them a percentage for every sale they make.

— Selling his product through Amazon, where the percentage take-home is smaller but there is a great window provided for sales on a global scale.

EXPERIENTIAL EVENT (TOUCHPOINT 05)

His experience could be to create a day seminar and invite small business entrepreneurs to understand "how to grow your business from the inside out". He could run a day workshop based on the key principles of his podcasts, and talk through the big mistakes that businesses make and the things they need to get right.

COLLABORATION (TOUCHPOINT 03)

He could partner with a group of successful entrepreneurs to speak on the day and offer their services. It is easy to Google different people who have written books on how to stay in business or build your business and ask them to speak and inspire on the day.

PRESS/DIGITAL AND PRINT (TOUCHPOINT 01)

This event could be a press launch in London, with a podcast taking place online to sell tickets both online and offline so anybody anywhere can livestream the information on the day. Although the press may have a front-row seat at the event you could also have a front-row seat in the comfort of your own home where you can type in your questions to be answered by the speakers throughout the day.

This event could be held once a year, to create a following with new speakers always hosting the event and a new box set, book or extra products being produced and sold to the target audience created to follow what he is telling them to do.

THESE TOUCHPOINT STRATEGIES CAN BE ADAPTED TO SUIT YOUR BUSINESS. THIS SHOULD GIVE YOU A GOOD BASE TO START GETTING CREATIVE WITH YOUR BUSINESS.

THE BEST PART OF ANY DAY FOR ME IS SITTING WITH A BUSINESS AND WORKING OUT THE JIGSAW PUZZLE TO SUPERSIZE THEIR BUSINESS AND LAUNCH THEM INTO THE REALM OF STAND-OUT STATUS. IF DONE RIGHT, ONE IDEA CAN ACHIEVE THIS OVERNIGHT AND YOU WILL BE LEFT SITTING THERE WONDERING HOW IT CAN BE SO EASY AND WHY ISN'T EVERYBODY ELSE DOING IT. YOU JUST NEED TO DEVELOP YOURSELF A CAN-DO ATTITUDE AND THE WORLD WILL BE YOUR OYSTER.

THIS FINAL TOUCHPOINT GOES HAND IN HAND WITH THE OTHER FOUR. THERE ARE OBVIOUS BENEFITS TO USING EACH ONE INDIVIDUALLY, AND YOU'LL MOST LIKELY SEE AN INCREASE IN YOUR EXPOSURE. HOWEVER, IT IS IMPERATIVE FOR YOU TO USE ALL FIVE TOUCHPOINTS IN SYNC WITH EACH OTHER IF YOU ARE REALLY GOING TO HIT #BRANDFAMOUS STAND-OUT STATUS.

THE BRANDS WHICH ULTIMATELY ACHIEVE STAND-OUT STATUS ARE THE ONES THAT USE THE FIVE TOUCHPOINTS IN A 360° WAY SO THAT YOU USE ALL THE ELEMENTS TOGETHER TO CREATE A FAR-REACHING CAMPAIGN. SO, BEFORE MOVING ON TO THE FINAL EVALUATE SECTION, LET'S PLAY A FINAL GAME TO ENSURE YOU ARE EMBRACING ALL FIVE TOUCHPOINTS.

GAME 02
CREATE YOUR TOUCHPOINT STORYBOARD

Using the five touchpoints together, collate all the information from the games above and write out what the story of your brand to market would look like. Reread the examples provided above and incorporate each touchpoint to launch the product/goal/target that you have highlighted. You can download the touchpoint storyboard from www.brandfamous.com/touchpoint-storyboard.

CREATE YOUR OWN TOUCHPOINT STORYBOARD

TOUCHPOINT 02

TOUCHPOINT 02

TOUCHPOINT 01

TOUCHPOINT 03

TOUCHPOINT 04

TOUCHPOINT 05

Now that you have put your touchpoint storyboard together, let's move on together and see how we can evaluate everything we have done in the final step of your journey towards stand-out fame. Come this way...

CHAPTER 13: STEP FIVE #EVALUATE

MEASURING YOUR SUCCESS AS A STAND-OUT BRAND

Congratulations on reaching the final step. You have put so much work into creating the ideas, producing the product, connecting it to retail and promoting it. So, how do you really know that all that hard work is paying off? Is there a way of actually "measuring success" so that it is not just guesswork or a wish and a prayer, but your brand is doing everything it is supposed to do? Why is it important to evaluate anyway?

You and I both know that this is the section that everybody dreads. I'd rather eat my own shoes, but over the years I have come to learn just how important it is and a part of me even leaps for joy when I have the figures laid out in front of me showing the results and achievements for all the efforts made. So if, like me, you would perhaps rather watch paint dry, let me at least help you through the evaluation process to ensure that the steps you are taking with your brand are going to:

— be beneficial for the brand,

— monetize the brand,

— and raise the profile of your brand.

Not evaluating your brand's progress is a little bit like working hard for an exam, then not bothering to find out the result. When I started Surgery all those years ago I didn't understand the evaluation process; I had to look up ROI and KPI to see what they stood for. None of the companies that I had worked with, large or small, had ever emphasized this in those

early days of business when we worked on putting their marketing and PR plans together. Thirteen years on, we provide a service where we have to deliver return on investment and key performance indicators for every piece of work that we do. In fact, we wouldn't be doing a responsible job for our clients if we did not have both of these markers in place. This applies to both the client and your own business as well.

My intention in this chapter is for you to see clearly why evaluating your brand is such an integral part of your brand journey. Without this piece of the pie, you will never know how close to or far from success you truly are. You might as well stick your finger in the air and fly by the seat of your pants. To be in a position to evaluate your brand, you will have to think about setting ROI and KPI targets in order to see if the projects you have delivered on have indeed been successful.

LINZIPEDIA: ROI – RETURN ON INVESTMENT

Return on investment is when you yield a beneficial return on what you have invested in the project. This does not always come back in direct monetary terms; it can be measured as the performance of the brand and awareness in the marketplace but more commonly it has a knock-on effect in relation to sales.

LINZIPEDIA: KEY PERFORMANCE INDICATOR

A measurement of performance; KPIs define and measure progress within your organization to achieve goals set. Once all the targets are in place, you need a way to measure progress towards those goals and this is where KPIs come in. They mean that you know on a month-by-month basis whether you are hitting your targets to get your ROI or not.

Over the years many people have mentioned that they find it hard to measure their success and deliver on expectations. Without a KPI in place it is impossible to know specifically what those expectations are and what somebody else in the business might perceive as a good or bad result. Imagine how different this could be if targets, budgets and goals are clearly defined at the beginning of each project and monitored throughout the project to ensure things are on track. Success is not only measured but also rewarded at the end of the project, when all expectations have been delivered upon. If I were to ask you to assess the different projects you are currently working on, would you know how well you are doing and what results you have actually achieved over the last year?

Setting targets and determining the return on your investments enables you and your team to deliver on projects and gauge their success. It's important to assess when things haven't worked and most importantly be able to investigate why so you can make the key changes that enable evolution and growth to take place within the brand. KPIs put in place reference points that enable you to compare one month with the next and, year on year, to check in and notice whether you are on track with your business plan and the projects you have laid out.

ROI is key to gauging whether the efforts poured into a project have reaped rewards. It enables you to look at the different aspects of the brands from brand awareness and data capture to the financial rewards which enable the brand to move on to the next phase of growth. Without knowledge of your ROI, how can you know how much money to invest in a particular area of your business?

THE ONLY WAY TO REALLY KNOW WHAT WORKS IS TO REFLECT ON WHAT YOU HAVE DONE IN THE PAST, LEARN FROM YOUR ACTIONS AND EVALUATIONS AND USE THIS KNOWLEDGE TO SET KPIs AND ROIs.

LET THE DOT-TO-DOT BEGIN:
EVALUATE YOUR BRAND

PLAY THE EVALUATE DOT-TO-DOT GAME

CREATE WHAT YOUR EXPERIENCE LOOKS LIKE

GAME 01A
MEASURE YOUR OVERALL BUSINESS GROWTH WITH ACHIEVABLE GOALS

GAME 01B
WRITE OUT YOUR OVERALL BUSINESS COST WITH KPIS AND ROI INCLUDED

GAME 02
COMPLETE YOUR BRAND FAME ROAD MAP WITH KPIS AND ROI INCLUDED

#EVALUATE

SETTING KPIs AND ROIs FOR YOUR BUSINESS – YOU CAN'T HAVE ONE WITHOUT THE OTHER

There are still many businesses setting KPIs and throwing hundreds of thousands of pounds at projects with no real awareness of what ROI they are looking to achieve. I find this alarming. Please don't be one of those businesses...

To reap the benefits of working to KPI with ROI, it's important to start today so you can instantly measure your results and know where, when and how to spend money on your business so that it is quantifiable and no longer about guesswork.

THE IMPORTANCE OF ROI

Creating the ROI for your whole plan reflects the budget that you have set aside to spend on the projects that you want to implement. I know that this can be a daunting process if you are in the build phase, for instance, unclear on how much spare money you may have, never mind what return on investment you think it will generate. Again, using the baby steps approach rather than no steps may be just what you need to get started.

This next comment could come as a shock. Ever since owning my first company, my personal mantra has always been "Don't allow money to stop you from doing anything" – I have to say it has always served me well. You might not have any money to spend on your dream project. So what? Your investment could be small but at least make sure that you know the possible return on that investment; if it's larger than what you put in then go for it. The goal is knowing what return you can realistically make and sensibly deciding how much you are willing to invest. Some companies invest millions. Do you think they would do that if they could not physically see a potential, possibly enormous, return on that investment?

Setting ROI enables you to have the confidence to spend money on projects that you may otherwise have avoided because you thought you lacked the money to spend in that area. In my experience it's not about lack of money, it's about knowing whether the money you put down on a project will come back in droves. That is not to say you can sit back and not do anything, your intention has to be there as if you had the money (create it, fake it...): the plan, the reason for doing it and the results that it will yield. The clearer you are, the less likely you will be to use money as an obstacle to stop you from doing something. You are now driving the vision to help the money find you more easily and quickly than it would have done before.

Whatever your stage of business – BUILD, RENOVATE OR REFRESH – there are certain things that you will be required to have in place:

— Something to sell is the first thing (e.g., a product or service).
— Someone to sell it to (a distribution channel).
— Marketing and PR to drive sales.

When working out the ROI for your projects, I would highly recommend that you take these three things into account, as without these it will prove very difficult to get going. If you have no idea how much money you have, or if indeed you don't have any money at all, then map out the dream scenario for getting your projects off the ground. Look at the most cost-effective way of making this happen so that you get it done to the best of your ability and do not compromise on look, quality or function.

Oddly enough, having worked with some of the biggest high-street brand names, they more often than not have come to the agency with next to no money to invest – and I sometimes mean £500 – to get a project off the ground. Being creative and having the drive to succeed are perfect ingredients to work out the projects that are going to give you the biggest return on your investment. You are also looking for an increase in your brand awareness, traffic driven through your distribution channel and loads of sales of your product so as to provide you with an income stream to work on the next product, service or project.

GAME 01A
MEASURE YOUR OVERALL BUSINESS
GROWTH WITH ACHIEVABLE GOALS

—

My intention for this section is to enable you to set your KPIs and ROI for all the different areas you have been working on throughout this book. By now you should have completed the games in each chapter so that you have a list of "to do's", an idea of the journey your brand is going on, a product vision map that allows you to see what direction you are heading in and a touchpoint storyboard to allow you to get creative in terms of communicating your brand message to the world. Now, let's set KPIs and expected ROI for each…

When setting KPIs and ROI, consider the following:

ARE THEY GOING TO GENERATE A RETURN ON MONEY?

ARE THEY GOING TO ENHANCE AWARENESS OF YOUR BRAND?

ARE THEY GOING TO CREATE HYPE AROUND YOUR BRAND?

WHAT DO YOU NEED TO DO TO ENSURE YOU MEET ALL TARGETS AND GUARANTEE THAT RETURN?

There will always be one or two things in each section that resonate with you, that you want to implement immediately. It is these things that we need to set KPIs for and work out your intended ROI. Below you will find a brand fame road map that showcases how this can be developed into phases of a critical path so that you can see how your own brand journey may take shape. Developing this enables you to be very specific about what you want to achieve at each step, allowing you to see growth in your business with results attached to success.

You must be clear about what you want to achieve from each step. You can set targets at three months, six months, nine months and one year (which can also be looked at as phases 1, 2, 3 and 4 for instance).

Before getting started

Take into account that the initial discover section is the area that I call "investing in your brand". It is the stage where you are laying the foundations so that you can build a sturdy house. It will not bring a return in monetary terms, yet it will bring the biggest intangible return of all the five step chapters as you have set the blueprint and foundations for your brand. If you are in the build phase it is the essential area to understand your brand and if you are in the renovate or refresh stage it enables you to reconnect with your brand and see what, where and how you want to position yourself moving forwards.

Setting your overall KPIs and ROI for the brand

The first requirement is to have an idea of your budget and how you will use it to get the biggest return possible so that you can generate your future income stream, which will enable you to work on the next stage of your project.

Imagine having four different areas of the business, which are priorities for achieving results in the coming six months. By mapping these out, your projection could show that they will generate an income to allow three more areas to develop in the second half of the year using the profit you will have achieved from the first four.

Here is a reminder of what you could pull out from the different steps of the #brandfamous process that you may wish to draw on when putting your own map together:

DISCOVER
— DEFINE THE BRAND ESSENCE, NEED, HABIT AND DESIRE
— BUILD/RENOVATE/REFRESH YOUR BRANDING

CREATE
— CREATE YOUR TOOLKIT (WEBSITE, BROCHURES, VIDEO, ETC.)
— CREATE YOUR PRODUCT

CONNECT
— MARKETS
— TERRITORIES
— DISTRIBUTION

COMMUNICATE
— PR/MARKETING
— SOCIAL MEDIA

For each of these sections, create a document and think about what your targets are for the next year. You should aim to formulate the following:
— What it is you want to achieve.
— When it should be completed by.
— How you are going to action it.
— Who is going to work on it to make it happen.

A costing sheet will then provide you with clarity on what your budget is and how the project can generate a return on your investment.

HOW TO SET KPIS AND ROI

In order for you to really understand how to use this process, I have provided you with an example of a business costing that has both KPIs and ROI attached to it so that you can see the process and be able to replicate it.

The following business costing is based on a brand that runs an offline education programme selling courses. It is interested in a second phase of teaching online, along with selling own products and white label products. The brand was eager to move on by creating own product lines and realized the need to recoup some money first to be able to take the business to stage two. Below you will find the road map of where the business needed to go to enable growth for the business in phase 1.

PHASE 1 PLAN – ROAD MAP

Discover, create, connect and communicate

Description	KPI	ROI
Discover Workshop	Define brand: — Point of difference — Need/habit — Target audience — Game	Investment
Create Toolkit	Promotional branding White label product	Awareness to drive traffic to product ×3 Sample sold on e-commerce site with expected sales of 50 on two styles (lower mark-up) and 5 on one style (higher costs)
Connect Website	Educational e-commerce	Sales from site (details below)
Communicate Marketing and PR	Courses and site	Listed below

The process I have mapped out is very much a sales and marketing drive, showing how to move into phases 2, 3 and 4 to make up the overall plan for the year. It can be drawn up for the purposes of your brand to show against investment in:
— The brand
— Product
— A campaign
— All three combined

" "

—

Most businesses fail because they want the right things but measure the wrong things and they get the wrong results

Gordon Bethune
Former CEO Continental Airlines

In order to achieve this first stage of growth, a brand needs to look at the targets that are being set, the initial investment to achieve these targets and the return on investment to enable the brand to move on to phase 2.

01 **KPIs** – the targets set to achieve a return on the investment made.
02 **Investment for development** – expenditure and fixed costs.
03 **ROI** – The actual return that comes from setting the KPIs and the money left over.

In order to know how to set the budget for phase 1 growth in the business, a brand needs to set their targets to see what areas they should be spending their money on to achieve a return on their investment. This should also enable them to evaluate phase 1 and the areas that were successful in order to then build upon them for phase 2 growth.

KPIS SET FOR LAUNCH OF BUSINESS PHASE 1

Drive 300 people to the site in three months.
Place Google ads to generate sales.
Write blogs about my courses to drive 100 people to the site.
Turn 20% of these people into sale.
Sell 100 items of product style 2 – white label.
Sell 5 items of product style 1 – white label.
Get 200 hits on the videos.
Drive traffic to the Facebook site.
Generate 100 likes on the fan page.

INVESTMENT OF FUNDS IN PHASE 1 OF PROJECT

Invest for development to bring money into phase 2 and grow the business:
Website development cost – £5000
Marketing – £1000
Video creation to promote courses and content – £1000
Brochure-type video – £800
PayPal acceptance – £100
SEO on site – £200 (page one of Google)
Branding for white label product – £485
Total cost of site – £8585

RETURN ON INVESTMENT (ACTUAL FIGURES) ONCE PHASE 1 COMPLETE

410 people went on the site in three months
90 people booked on the course
Course price £180/person for level 1, with people then being driven to levels 2 to 4

Profit of £16,200
180 likes on the Facebook site
76 items of interest on the site – profit/item £19;
total = £1444
8 high-priced white label items – profit/item £427;
total = £3416

Total amount generated £21,060

Money spent on phase 1

Website costs	£8585
Business fixed costs and overheads	£3760
Discovery session	£500
Branding costs and toolkit	£1500
Total costs	**£14,345**
Money left over after costs met	£671

The return on investment for this was strong and proven in a number of different areas.

ROI for phase 1

— The assets are now in place to be able to drive more sales from the site onto the course and product lines.
— There is potential to sell higher-level courses to those people that came on the first course.
— A profit was shown even after all the setup costs had been put in place for the brand.
— Testing of white label product sold well, with further areas of growth after this period.

Going through this exercise in phase 1 enabled the brand to assess the first stage of growth and set the milestones for growth in the second phase of business development.

SECOND PHASE OF GROWTH FOR THE BUSINESS
___

Assessing the first stage of growth and the milestones set enabled this business to:
— Sell further courses through the online programme.
— Invest more in marketing to sell courses and product; look at a creative campaign.
— Create their own product line using the ever-growing database built up on their site to test before ordering.
— Set up a pop-up clinic allowing the consumer to experience their service first hand.

They set aside some of their profits each month to put towards these developments so they were able to grow the business and invest in this second phase of growth.

In phase 1 the white label products were only sold to their B2B customers who then sold them on to their customers; however, the products they went on to create themselves attracted B2C customers and thus widened their distribution outreach by selling to a very large shopping channel.

WRITE OUT YOUR OVERALL BUSINESS COSTS WITH KPIS AND ROI INCLUDED

—

DESCRIPTION	AMOUNT	KPI	ROI

DISCOVER

CREATE

CONNECT

COMMUNICATE
— Print
— Social
— Retail
— Partnerships
— Experiential events

When working out your ROI, always consider the return you want to get from the project as well as the outcome that will best deliver on your quest for brand fame. Are you creating an e-commerce site to sell product along with a TV channel to showcase video content to raise awareness of the brand and drive traffic to the site and the services that you offer? Alternatively, are you using a website as a platform for case studies of work, with testimonials and updated video content, which you can manage and where you can highlight your work – updated on a regular basis – to generate interest and ultimately business from your YouTube channel with fresh new content.

Keep checking your progress
Once the projects are up and running, you will need to analyse if you are hitting your targets. Are you over or under the targets you set and how does this affect your ROI? Also, try to make sure that you stay out of the red and in the black with the costs that you have incurred. If one of your objectives was to create awareness and get new business from the website, what exactly has been the outcome and how much money has this generated in new business leads that have turned into transactions?

Assessment – end of each phase

The objectives you set at the beginning of each phase will give you clear guidance on whether you are hitting your targets and what areas you need to look at improving to enable sustainable growth. You should be able to assess via your online platform what has been the uptake from, for example, word of mouth and what percentage came directly from your marketing and social media campaigns or website. You should then be able to determine the exact return on your investment.

You can do this by looking at the amount of money you have spent on your project or website and relate it to the amount of sales that have come through the website/distribution channel. Also, assess through your online and print coverage what awareness and traffic have been brought to the brand. In this way something you initially thought was expensive could in fact become incredibly accessible in comparison when you see the benefits it has brought to your business.

Next time you look to update the site you will have a measurable result to base this on, so that you will know what percentage of money to spend in this particular area.

If, in contrast, the project has generated neither income nor awareness (i.e. no ROI at all) then you will know that the project has not worked and you need to re-evaluate the site to see what changes can be made so that you do get the ROI that you are looking for next time around.

Once you have determined your overall plan with your KPIs set you must remember to update the targets on a monthly basis and make sure you stay on track.

Setting your budget

It does not matter how much budget you have, as any one of the projects could feed the others. If you have £5000 set aside you may want to use this to create your website, a promotional video and sample product line to sell on the site along with some creative thinking to promote your product and website (as listed in the communication section).

LB SUGGESTS

—

There are now some great "off-the-shelf" e-commerce sites you can buy for approximately £100 and then employ a graphic designer to skin the site and make it fit your branding.

EVALUATE YOUR BRAND THROUGH A SPIKE

Now you have taken a good look at your overall plan, let's look at what happens when it comes to evaluating the launch of a special project or a limited edition range. Creating two plans – the one above and this one – will enable you to be flexible and creative with your execution of a project or a spike (as mentioned in the communicate section; touchpoint 5) so that the plan is developed as and when it is needed depending on what/when you are about to launch. This is much more flexible and can be dropped in at any time throughout the year as long as your budget permits

In the plan for your brand laid out above, you are able to work on fixed costs and targets that are there to create growth in your business year on year – tangible costs which create a platform to execute ideas and product that is moving with your business dependent on what is happening at the time. A creative project or something that is limited edition or short term is there to spike your brand awareness within the marketplace and create a platform to achieve stand-out status away from the normal execution of most business.

Creating your project KPI

Variable plan

The five Ps:

Promotional material

Projects that are changeable on a seasonal basis

Pop-up stores

Products or services (limited edition)

Partnership collaborations

When writing your plan for a creative concept, look at the five Ps to help you engage with your consumer and speak to them in the most creative way that is relevant to your core values. Looking at the five Ps will enable you to inject life into your business and give it a point of difference that will create the awareness that you desire to move away from the fixed costs that you are used to. Your cash flow projection will require these costs to be included in the overall plan with a cost structure defined so that you are able to get creative and look at how the ROI will be achieved from these projects. Bear in mind that one of these creative concepts may be the thing that escalates your brand to stand-out status; however, the fixed cost strategy is the thing that ties everything together so that you have a solid platform for your business to grow from. You cannot have one without the other and both provide the ROI that you require to have spikes and growth within your business.

The project KPIs are always set on the basis of launching something new in a creative way.

GAME 02
COMPLETE YOUR BRAND FAME ROAD MAP WITH KPIS AND ROI INCLUDED

Brand fame project road map

DESCRIPTION	KPI	ROI
PROMOTIONAL MATERIAL		
PROJECT		
POP-UP STORE		
LIMITED EDITION PRODUCT		
PARTNERSHIP COLLABORATION		
PRINT (NUMBER OF PIECES OF COVERAGE)		
ONLINE COVERAGE		
SOCIAL (LIKES, RE-TWEETS)		

External KPI: How an external project can validate success

I mentioned that we work on the same process for our clients as we do for our own business – working with over 30 businesses at one time we set a strategy with measurable results so that both the agency and the client can set targets to achieve their long-term plan and evaluate year on year a growth pattern within their business. We have to write set targets for external businesses that we work with. You need to see which category your client sits in and work project by project, or maybe your business structure is set up so that you can write a standard plan which can be reworked on a six-monthly basis by just revisiting the set targets and not recreating new ideas.

Whatever happens, I suggest that you have measurable targets for everyone that you work with so that you are both clear on where you started and where you have arrived at in the working period together. It is great to then be able to measure your success and track the highs and lows so that you can revisit the circumstances for success and failure and monitor the situation. This also provides both parties with a reference so that when a new team starts to work on the account they have full understanding of where the client has been and what has taken place. Remember, where there is a will, there is a way – just take that step; life has a funny way of providing you with the things that you need most to make any project happen.

EXAMPLE WORK BOOK FOR CREATING YOUR KPI PLAN

Toolkit creation
Getting started – create a new toolkit:
— Website, videos, brochure.
— Look at your branding and see if it needs updating.

Updating your toolkit
— Write out set targets that you will stick with to update your toolkit.
— Who will update the website on a daily/weekly/ monthly basis?

PR/marketing
Getting started – create a list of places where you can promote your product/services:
— Write out a press release.
— Prepare a biography on yourself.
— Take a profile picture.
— Prepare e-shots for new product alerts that you want to send out.

Social media
— Create a Facebook, Twitter, Instagram, YouTube and Pinterest account.
— Update these on a daily/weekly basis.
— Write out a social media plan. You can write down all of the things that you would like to do in the next year/even three years and then work backwards so that it goes into a micro plan.

Territories

This looks at how many offices you have and within which territories. You may not be trading out of anywhere at the moment, or you could have one office in the UK. Opening up multiple offices in different territories may enable you to:
— Open up an office in your country.
— Open up an office in multiple countries.
— Create one or multiple new divisions.

Markets

Looking at which markets you sell in at the moment; you may only have one.

Product

Which products/services do you want to create? A building product, DVD box set, clothing range, etc. How can you track the product sales? This will reflect on your distribution channel through online and in-store activity.

Distribution

— What distribution channels are you looking at?
— Create an amount every six months that you can track and monitor. The toolkit creation will play a part in evaluating the ROI so that you can monitor if this has created an awareness around selling in your product.

Winning new business

— Setting budgets.
— Getting creative with your toolkit.

QUICK PEEK (HEAT SHEET

—

WHAT WE HAVE EVALUATED

01 SETTING KPIs AND ROIs FOR YOUR BUSINESS
YOU CAN'T HAVE ONE WITHOUT THE OTHER

—

02 THE IMPORTANCE OF KPI
KNOW WHY YOU REQUIRE KPIs IN YOUR
BUSINESS

—

**03 MEASURE YOUR OVERALL BUSINESS GROWTH
WITH ACHIEVABLE GOALS**
MAKE SURE YOU KNOW WHAT YOU ARE
MEASURING

—

04 HOW TO SET KPIs AND ROIs
PLANNING YOUR ROAD MAP

—

**05 WRITE OUT YOUR OVERALL BUSINESS COSTS
WITH KPI AND ROI**
KEEP CHECKING THE UPDATE/RESULTS

—

06 EVALUATE YOUR BRAND THROUGH A SPIKE
CREATING YOUR PROJECT PLAN

—

**07 COMPLETE YOUR BRAND FAME ROAD MAP
WITH KPI AND ROI INCLUDED**
EXAMPLE WORKBOOK FOR CREATING YOUR KPI
PLAN

—

Enter your information at the school of brand fame to gain
more insight and also a game summary.
www.brandfamous.com/schoolofbrandfame

WELCOME TO THE WORLD OF STAND-OUT

You have finally made it! Everybody loves you, wants to be you, is talking about you, writing about you, you are absolutely in the limelight and can do no wrong. You are basking in your own glory; you know you have made it as you have a big tick next to each one the following:

— Everyone is talking about you.
— Celebrities are wearing/using your product
— Retailers are desperate to buy your brand
— Magazines are all writing about you
— People are wanting to partner with you
— You are a market leader in your area of expertise

You can do no wrong. Or can you?

Stand-out is the status that everyone tries to achieve and yet so many brands fail to sustain their status. Why do you think that over the years I have worked with so many brands that have lain dormant, desperate to exceed their former glory. They all once had stand-out status and have known the taste of success. However, when in that former glory they were totally unaware that they needed to work on sustaining and increasing their status, instead of just sitting back.

People and brands are so unaware that there will ever be a shift in trends when they are sitting on their thrown, they are oblivious to the fact that times are always changing and so must they. There are only a few giants in this world that operate on a level – as I mentioned in the beginning to this book – where they realize that the way to stay stand-out is to constantly shift and evolve.

Nike and Apple are both pioneers of change, you would never realize it as a consumer but their internal machine is always creating and evolving so that they are ahead of the game and are reinventing to stay at the forefront of their industry – they embrace a life of inner and outer beauty and create a process to always attract the most creative ways of executing that so everyone around them is a part of the experience. They have no problem in going back to the incubator time and time again to always come out on top.

The world is an evolving place and you must evolve also, to create the impossible and never stop. No one is going to drive your brand except you. That is why passion, excitement and commitment have to be the primary drivers of any business – love work and love your brand. Infuse the passion into the brand that will ignite others working on it. Inspire people to create the impossible and generate a leadership quality so that everyone working in the brand feels like they are working on the brand.

YOU CAN NEVER STAND STILL; YOU ALWAYS NEED TO CHALLENGE, ASSESS AND CREATE TO PROVIDE YOUR BRAND WITH A NEW WAY TO BE A PIONEER WITHIN YOUR SECTOR. DID YOU HONESTLY THINK YOU COULD STAND STILL? DID YOU THINK THAT STAND-OUT MEANT COMPLETION? IT IS LIKE ANYTHING IN LIFE, ONCE YOU REACH YOUR DESTINATION YOU LOOK TO THE NEXT NEW CHALLENGE.

SHARE THE VISION **AND CREATE THE POSSIBILITY OF** GOING OVER AND ABOVE **WHAT PEOPLE THINK CAN HAPPEN. YOU CAN ALWAYS** REACH FOR PLACES THAT YOU NEVER THOUGHT WERE POSSIBLE **IF YOU OPEN YOUR MIND UP TO THE POSSIBILITY THAT MAYBE YOU CAN** CREATE SOMETHING TRULY GROUNDBREAKING...

ACKNOWLEDGEMENTS

___

The three most important people to whom I dedicate this book...

Kai and Isla my beloved children; Isla was only 4 months old when I started writing this book. They have both provided me with the space to learn to juggle being both a working mum and an active mum – I love you so much.

To Gary my beautiful husband/silent subeditor without whom this book would not have made nearly as much sense – he is always my support and allows me to always be me. You make it all possible.

Special thanks to...

Mum and dad who set me on my path when I was 18 and helped me with my first shop and have been there ever since.

My two brothers Philip and Iain – growing up with them made me be able to be one of the girls and one of the boys. I am so happy to have had two older brothers.

Caroline Gautier, for sticking with me for over a decade and being like two peas in a pod.

Chris Connors (Robin) who has been there from the start and my constant.

Debbie Wosskow – from age 12 we still grow.

Ruth Parish – you always inspire me with your strength.

Mike Weeks – so funny, you specifically sat on my shoulder whilst I edited this book.

Bean Sopwith whom I treasure.

Tara Dakin Pollard, my true sister who "predicted" I would write this book a long time ago.

You are all my life friends.

Frankie Kitson – behind every great women is another set of helping hands!

Surgery and the many people that I have had the pleasure to work with – you have been as much my growth and source of knowledge as I hope I have been yours.

Darren Shirlaw and Paul Stead – for finding my new path, I am happy to walk down it with the both of you

Wiley – for believing in me and publishing this book.

The look and feel of the book
Rankin – who I have known for so very long, I am honoured to be added to your iconic repertoire of portraits.

ico design and Vincent Howcutt – without you this book would not have looked nearly as fabulous.

Roland Mouret – I have worn and loved your dresses since you began and their was only one choice of dress for me to wear when shooting the cover.

Never forgetting
An industry that I have worked in since the age of 15 – I have grown up with you, you have held my hand, shown me the way, nurtured me, watched me grow and graduate from the school of life. I have met some incredible people, retail owners, editors of magazines, heads of brands and other fellow media types. Thank you, you have been my friends that I have learnt from and I am still forever learning...

WHATEVER YOUR INTENTIONS WERE IN READING THIS BOOK – I HOPE YOU HAVE ENJOYED AND TAKEN SOMETHING FROM IT. IF YOU ARE WONDERING "WHAT'S NEXT?" OR "WHAT MORE IS THERE?"

I WOULD LIKE TO INVITE YOU TO TAKE PART IN...

The School of
BRAND
FAME

Imagine if you could experience this book live from the comfort of your home with Linzi Boyd and her team of experts teaching you first hand the tricks and techniques that have been written about in this book

To get you started there is a downloadable Discover your brand poster that takes you on the journey to uncovering your brand essence quicker

To download it, you are one click away from
www.schoolofbrandfame.com

For all other brand fame information and social media chit chat please find us on
www.brandfamous.com

Tweet along with @Linzi_Boyd

Find out who is twittering on @Brand_Famous

Facebook
www.facebook.com / LinziBoyd
www.facebook.com / BrandFamous

Instagram Linzi Boyd

ABOUT THE AUTHOR

Linzi Boyd left school at 15 and went from working in a clothes shop to opening one of her own by the age of 18. Linzi bought Replay and Diesel in Paris and Milan, launching them into the North of England, before selling the shop, aged 20 to set up a footwear brand with a successful shoe designer. Stride sold 150,000 pairs in the first season through 7 global distribution channels, the shoes were featured in the design museum as design classics next to Evian bottles, and were worn by Robbie Williams and the Beastie boys.

The shoe company was sold to Caterpillar when she was 24 and Linzi went on to set up Surgery PR, which has since developed into Surgery Group over-seeing 7 different businesses focused on building, renovating and refreshing brands. Surgery Group, one of London's leading communication agencies, has worked with Marc Newson, Superdry, G-Star, Alexa Chung for Superga, Wrangler, Pringle, Urban Outfitter, Rankin, Aldo, Desigual, Lacoste, Givenchy eyewear, Tinie Tempah for Disturbing London amongst many more globally established brands and campaigns.

Thereafter, Midas and the School of Brand Fame were immediately launched. Midas, a business which specialises in creating long-term value for celebrities, brands and business leaders currently works with A-list entrepreneurs and VIPs. The School of Brand Fame, which will open up its doors in late 2014 will offer on and offline courses for SMEs. Full access into the complete methodology will be taught whilst her Young Entrepreneur Scheme (YES) will run alongside Surgery Group providing an ability for school leavers who wish to gain work experience alongside some of the most recognisable brands – providing mentorship and experience, something Linzi wished she had access to when leaving school at such a young age.

Linzi has appeared on several TV shows and segments, including *Say No to the Knife*, which she presented, and regular appearances on BBC Breakfast and Channel 4.

NOTES

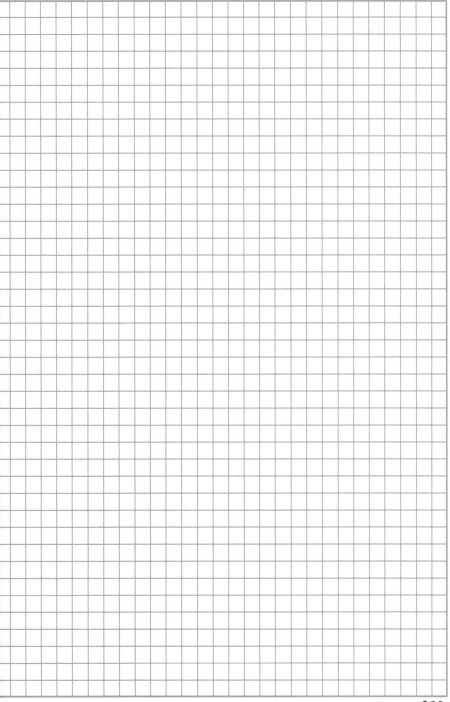

NOTES

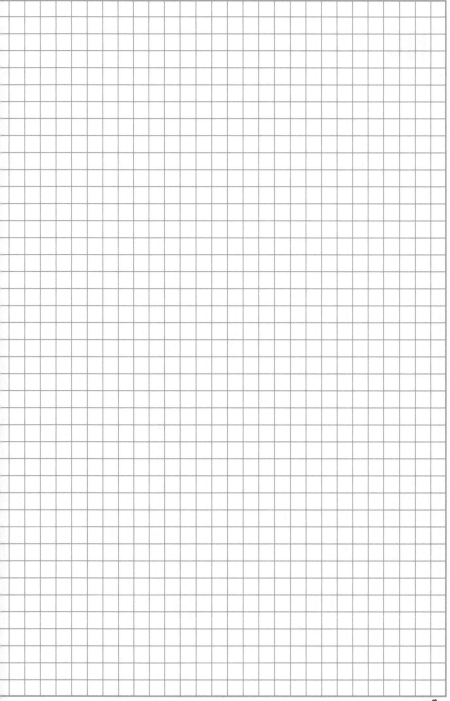

NOTES

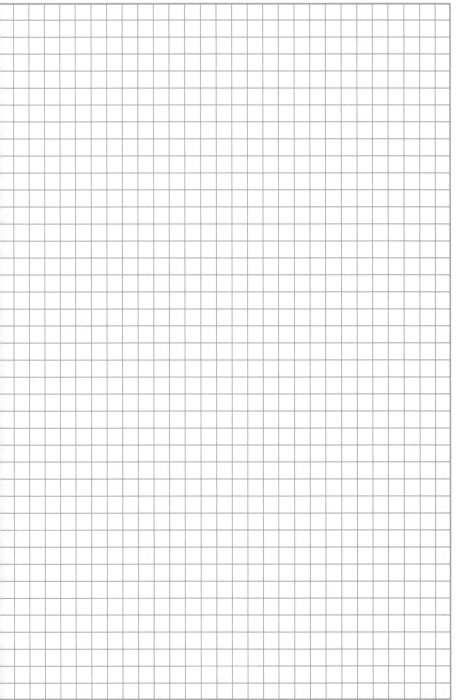

NOTES

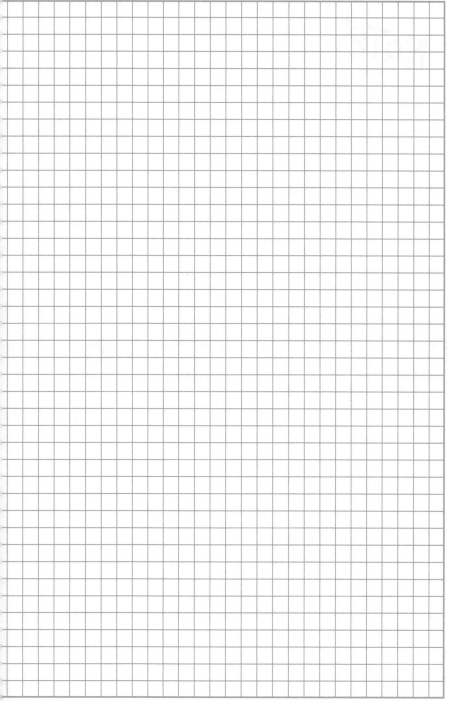

285

NOTES

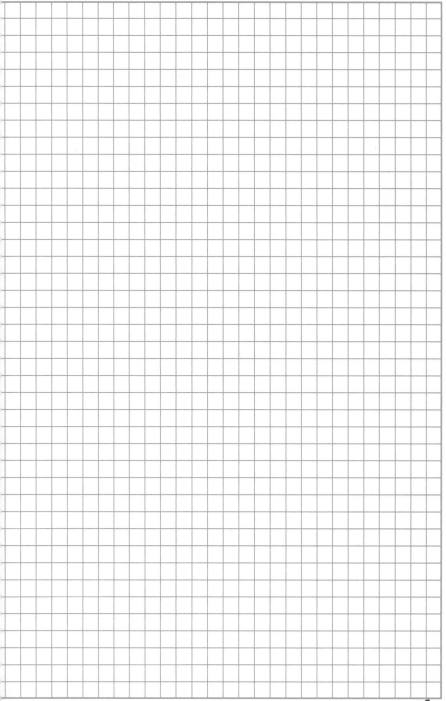